Risk In Perspective

Risk In Perspective

Insight and Humor in the Age of Risk Management

Dr. Kimberly M. Thompson

AORM
P.O. Box 590129
Newton Centre, MA 02459
www.aorm.com

Notice

The information in this book is designed to help you think, laugh, and make more informed decisions about your health and life's risks. It is not intended as a substitute for any treatment prescribed by your doctor. Oscar Wilde's observation that "A poet can survive everything but a misprint" may apply more broadly to those who read health books. If you suspect that you have a medical problem then seek competent medical help, and take your sense of humor.

Published in 2004 by AORM (Newton Centre, MA)

Printed in the United States of America on acid-free paper.

Library of Congress Control Number: 2004105591

ISBN 0-9727078-2-4 (paperback)

Visit the Age of Risk Management web site at www.aorm.com

To my wonderful parents, Drs. Billie M. Thompson and Kirk D. Thompson, in honor of their 60th birthdays, with enormous thanks for teaching me the joy of laughter, the power of well-spoken words, and about the 3 C's (Communication, Certainty, and Commitment).

Acknowledgments

I thank my parents for introducing me to famous quotations, great books, and "funnies," and for a wonderful childhood full of laughs and good times. I appreciate their support of my lifelong learning, high expectations, and constant encouragement to make good choices. This book celebrates the first 60 years of each of their lives.

I thank Kamran, Nima, and Deanna for their continued love, support, and patience, and for laughing along with me in this great adventure.

This book would not exist without the amazing talents of artists who so eloquently capture concepts in cartoons that are impossible to otherwise capture, even with 1,000 or more words. I thank them for making me laugh, for their insight, courage, honesty, creativity, integrity, hard work, and most of all for allowing this compilation to exist.

I thank John Ahearne, Denny Bier, Sam Brownback, Bill Deane, Sharon Dunwoody, Sidney Harris, Carden Johnston, Joe Lieberman, George Lundberg, Howard Raiffa, Sylvia Rowe, June Walker, Elizabeth Whelan, and Tom Zender for their kind words for the book jacket. I thank Neil Shulman for his gracious foreword and for recommending this book to every doctor in America. I thank Michael, Rick, Myron, Bill, Alan, Jim, Ed, Karen, Laura, Harriet, Chris, and David for comments, suggestions, and encouragement. I thank the Steering Committee members of the Health Insight Project, Christine Brunswick, John Cox, Betty Parsons Dooley, John Graham, Clarita Herrera, Rena Large, Marjorie Lightman, Ann Mason, and Joy Johnson-Wilson, for supporting my use of cartoons in the Consumer's Guide to Taking Charge of Health Information that paved the way for this book. I also thank the members of the Advisory Council for the Health Insight project for insisting that the guide become a book: Lauren Asher, Cheryl Beversdorf, Jonca Bull, Diane Camper, Kathryn Stern Ceja, Neena Chaudhry, Sheila Clark, Sol del Ande Eaton, Jonas Ellenberg, Christine Gould, Millicent Gorham, Anne Harvey, Susan Holleran, Liz Joyce, Annette Kane, Wendy Katz, Lynne Lackey, Kristen LaRose, Kia Lewis, Sherry Llewellyn, Irene Malbin, Sherry Marts, Walter McLeod, Dale Mintz, Rhonda Oziel, Roberta Rubin, Randy Wentsel, and Carole Zimmerman. I thank the Chlorine Chemistry Council for supporting the Health Insight Project, and Jeff Sloan and Leland Vincent for help in getting cartoon permissions. I thank Robert Donin, Kathy Mercier, Anne Taylor, Raegan Carmona, Chris Cassatt, Jim Cavett, and Meredith Miller for their help. I thank the students at the Harvard School of Public Health who've made teaching and mentoring an enormous pleasure, and who continue to inspire and teach me. I thank the many others who touched my life as part of my journey and synthesis of these materials over the past 15 years whose names would fill many pages.

And finally I thank you, the reader, for bringing this book along with you as you take charge of your health in the Age of Risk Management. I hope that this book will help empower you to ask better questions about your health, make better health choices, and enjoy a few moments of what is often called the best medicine - laughter.

Contents

Preface

This book aims to empower you to ask better questions about your health, make better health choices, and enjoy learning about risk. It contains a collection of quotes and cartoons that I accumulated over the last decade as a practicing risk analyst (which includes the roles of risk perceiver, assessor, manager, and communicator - see the classic cartoon by Sidney Harris below). While I considered what seems like an infinite number of ways to organize this book, in the end I decided on chapters based on themes. Each chapter begins with an introduction, a collection of quotes on the theme (you'll note that my large academic ego always lets me get the last word!), and a selection of what I consider to be relevant cartoons.

This book is assembled with the ambition of Nietzsche who said: "It is my ambition to say in ten sentences what others say in a whole book" and with appreciation of Mark Twain's insight that "few things are harder to put up with than a good example." For me, humor makes living in the Age of Risk Management much more fun. I hope that you will enjoy this book in the spirit in which it has been assembled, and that you will share my appreciation of the wisdom of some timeless words and the amazing work of some of the best contemporary cartoon artists who have captured this age so eloquently. I invite you to send me copies of other quotes and cartoons that you think also fit in, along with any comments, and to enjoy the adventure.

Kimberly M. Thompson, Sc.D.
December 2003

Foreword

As a physician, I know the serious side of medicine only too well. In my own interactions with patients I never forget the critical importance of showing and appreciating my humanity. I believe in using absolutely every communication tool available to reach out to patients, because communication is the foundation of the medical relationship between patient and doctor. While this point is seriously underemphasized in medical schools, optimal care depends on doctors understanding their patients' health, values, and preferences and working with them. Studies that show the critical need for good doctor-patient communication highlight the following:

- primary care physicians who never experienced a malpractice suit spend an average of 3.3 minutes more with patients, and they use more patient-centered interviewing techniques including humor,

- patients feel more satisfied when they believe doctors are addressing their concerns (that is to say, when they feel that their doctors listen to them), and

- less litigation is aimed at clinicians who have good communication skills (although it is not clear whether this results from fewer errors or better relationships or both).

In spite of the recognition of communication as one of the most important ingredients in high-quality health care, it remains one of the largest challenges and most significant impediments to empowering patients to embrace their roles as partners with physicians. However, the fact that something is difficult does not justify or excuse failing to pursue the goal.

Enter this truly unique book, *Risk in Perspective: Insight and Humor in the Age of Risk Management*. Dr. Kimberly Thompson, a skilled risk analyst and faculty member at the Harvard School of Public Health who manages to effectively speak to audiences at any level while talking about risk, tackles this challenge with a truly innovative approach. In this book, she provides quotes and cartoons that will help get you thinking and asking questions. This is a book that belongs in every physician's waiting room, and one that all Americans should read as they face and make daily decisions related to their health.

While not all of the examples relate directly to health, the analogies are clear. I suspect that the same is true for health-related examples when it comes to managing business and other types of risk. We are all risk managers, and we all benefit from the ability to step back and laugh. This book may seem too simple to be powerful, but it should not be underestimated. This book holds the power to teach you remarkable lessons as you laugh yourself silly – lessons that will improve your life and empower you to make better choices. I encourage you to enter a new stage in your life as an active decision maker in the Age of Risk Management by taking the plunge into the humorous and lighter side contained in the pages that follow. Remember that life is just a dash between two numbers on a tombstone.

Neil Shulman, M.D.
March 2003

Introduction

Many people already appreciate that we're living in the Age of Risk Management - a time in human history where we recognize that life is full of risks, choices often involve tough trade-offs, and good data and risk analysis play a critical role in the decisions we make as individuals and collectively. The Age of Risk Management brings with it a requirement for everyone to understand risks, deal with uncertainty, and remain ready, willing, and committed to making good choices.

I'm not just talking about professionals. I really mean everyone.

In my job as Associate Professor of Risk Analysis and Decision Science at the Harvard School of Public Health, I identify and assess all types of health risks, look for ways to deal with them, and find strategies to talk to people effectively about what they mean. Of course I realize that effectively managing health risks is a requirement for survival for all humans. Yet, in daily life in our roles as children, parents, students, teachers, employers, policy makers, workers, and so on, the dizzying array of risks that we face can be somewhat overwhelming if we don't keep the risks in perspective. Understanding the risks and keeping them in perspective for me makes the world much bigger, smaller, more manageable, and funnier, all at the same time. No matter who you are or what you do, take a minute to think about the risks in your daily life.

Consider some questions to help you think about your daily risks....

1. What risks do you face associated with everyday activities like eating, sleeping, and moving around? Balance this by remembering the benefits of these activities!

2. How have the risks that you've faced changed with time given choices that you've made? For example, consider risks you experienced when you were younger compared to your risks now.

3. How have your risks changed with time given the evolution of science and technology and the choices made by others (both individual and societal)?

4. What health-protective behaviors reduce your risks (like eating a balanced and nutritious diet, exercising regularly, and managing a chronic illness well)?

5. What health-threatening behaviors increase your risks (like eating too much, smoking, drinking excessively, abusing substances, or working in a high-stress job)?

6. What risks might you face if you stop working or significantly change where you spend your time? Remember the financial impacts and where you spend time both affect your identity.

7. What specific risks might you face on the job? Consider your understanding about these and whether you choose to actively take the opportunities that exist to reduce them.

Just by thinking about your own daily risks, you're getting some training in one part of risk analysis: **risk perception**. Willa Cather stated that "The history of every country begins in the heart of a man or woman." Similarly, the perception of risk begins in the mind of a woman or man. Risk perception involves using your senses, but it also frequently depends on powerful scientific and technological tools that allow us to measure beyond what we can sense alone. Today's scientific tools empower us not only with acute abilities to detect risks, but also with the necessary means of creating strategies for managing them.

Perceiving a risk may provide the motivation for beginning the process of attempting to understand and measure it, and for entering another part of risk analysis: **risk assessment**. The risk assessment process focuses on answering three questions:

1. What can happen (i.e., possibilities)?
2. How likely are these outcomes (i.e., probabilities)?
3. If these outcomes occur what are the consequences (i.e., impacts)?

As you can see, risk assessors ask a lot of questions. They deal with data and numbers. Risk assessors must synthesize the existing information, and consider sources of variability (i.e., the real differences that exist within a population that make generalization difficult) and uncertainty (i.e., all the pesky stuff that we don't know). Yet ultimately risk assessors must integrate the best available scientific knowledge into mathematical models, produce the best answers they can, and consider the world of "what-ifs." Thus, risk assessors must be wise in the sense intended by William James who said: "The art of being wise is the art of knowing what to overlook," but they must also be transparent so that those who depend on the results can understand all of the key assumptions and see any errors.

Another part of risk analysis, **risk communication**, focuses on finding effective ways to explain and talk about risk assessment results and put them into context in an effort to engage stakeholders in the process of managing the risk. Edith Wharton noted that "There are two ways of spreading light: to be the candle or the mirror that reflects it." In today's world, in which information spreads globally in fractions of seconds, communicators face the enormous challenges of engaging multiple parties in meaningful dialogue and rising above the clutter.

Ultimately decisions must be made, because even not taking action represents a choice. As Raold Dahl wrote: "You'll never get anywhere if you go around what-iffing like that. Would Columbus have discovered America if he'd said 'What if I sink on the way over? What if I meet pirates? What if I never come back?' He wouldn't even have started!" Thus, the process of **risk management** involves decision makers weighing the trade-offs of different options, deciding on any additional information needs and the value of information, and making choices. You manage your own risks at the individual level depending on your perceptions and assessments of risks, your preferences and values, and the options available to you. You should recognize that your options may be constrained by your resources, the society you live in, or other factors, and that your options may differ from the options faced by others. In the field of public health we often face risk management challenges that balance the societal benefits of actions against the costs to some individuals within the society (for example, consider vaccines or motor vehicle restraints).

Risk management also occurs at the organizational or societal level. Companies manage risks in many ways including testing their products, implementing quality control measures, and providing instructions and warning labels (which you should get in the habit of reading, by the way). The government manages risks by passing laws and making policies designed to protect consumers, and ideally by creating incentives for markets to function properly such that free choice prevails.

In theory, all involved work together to make sure that the right, relevant, and important questions get asked, and that the answers get communicated effectively. In practice, risk analysis is a new field and some bumps remain. Our ability to work together reflects the current state of our world, with all of the complexities that come from mixing up normal human interactions with uncertain science, complicated rules of law, differing values, and so on. The words of J.K. Rowling ring true: "It is our choices... that show what we truly are, far more than our abilities."

When I talk about the Age of Risk Management, I often give examples of familiar risks, like airbags, obesity, and smoking, and of more exotic risks, like new diseases. While I can always expand on any list of risks forever, I usually stop with what is often my biggest fear at that moment — simple things like spilling my cranberry juice down the front of my suit, falling off of the podium, or saying something stupid in front of hundreds of really smart people. Enormous advancements of science and technology empower us in the Age of Risk Management by providing high-quality information about risks and a spectrum of management choices. However, they also provide an overwhelming amount of health information (typified for me by the Jim Borgman cartoon that appears on the cover) that is often difficult to put into context. Most people see the everyday choices that they face. They deal with the reality of inevitable mortality, the solutions that create new problems, and the challenges of keeping up with life moving at the speed of "24/7." We do our best by muddling through.

This book started with recognition that we can often do better than simply muddling through, and that risk analysts need to play a critical role in helping people take charge of health information and empowering them to make better health choices. We absolutely must become better consumers when it comes to public and our own private health. Poverty, obesity, disease, violence, substance misuse, and injuries threaten the length and quality of our lives. It's time that we put the public back into public health. While many sources of information recognize their important roles in shaping people's perceptions, attitudes, and behaviors related to health, most consumers are on their own as they evaluate health information, put it into context, and make decisions about risk. By now you should realize that the concept of risk is important because it implies that there is some chance that something bad might happen. However, risk and uncertainty are not necessarily bad. While uncertainty can be frustrating and frightening, it also means that your attitude and choices can play a major role in your future health. Thus, risk implies opportunity. Once your recognize that you do have choices and that your choices matter, the best advice you might get when it comes to making sense of health information may be:

ASK QUESTIONS!

The next section provides a guide to get you started.

Health Insight: A Consumer's Guide to Taking Charge of Health Information

The following 10 questions are designed to help you take charge of health information and educate yourself about health risks and your opportunities to reduce risks. If you like detective novels, then consider these questions to be the tools that will help you turn health information into clues and get you started on becoming your own health risk detective.

1. What is the message?
Get past the presentation and to the facts. Consider that:
- Sources personalize information to make it more interesting, but not everyone relates to the same things.
- Your perception of information can depend on whether it is presented as positive (half-full) or negative (half-empty). Flipping the statements and looking for alternative ways to state them might change your perception. For example, if you hear about a small number of people being affected, remember that this means a large number are not affected, and vice versa.
- When the facts seem confusing, keep in mind that you might have been given false or incomplete information or you may have misunderstood the information given.

2. Is the source reliable?
Information comes from many sources, good and bad. Think about the information's quality. Consider that:
- All sources have a motivation for providing information. Try to identify the source and its funding so that you can consider any possible biases. The fact that a source or its source of money may benefit from the information does not necessarily mean that the information is false.
- Health information can be based on untested claims, anecdotes, case reports, surveys, and scientific studies. Scientific studies, which take samples and apply the results to the whole population, often provide the best clues about health. Nonetheless, many studies are needed to be confident about an answer. Below are some factors that might help you judge the information:

Less reliable (less certain)	More reliable (more certain)
One or a few observations	Many observations
Anecdote or case report	Scientific study
Unpublished	Published and peer-reviewed
Not repeated	Reproduced results
Nonhuman subjects	Human subjects
Results not related to hypothesis	Results about tested hypothesis
No limitations mentioned	Limitations discussed
Not compared to previous results	Relationship to previous studies discussed

It is important to read between the lines. Look for the assumptions that make the observations relevant to other members of the population. For example, do you have to assume that the same effects occur in humans as in rats? in women as in men? in children as in adults? These types of assumptions raise questions about how well the conclusions from the sample apply to the larger population. They do not necessarily mean that the conclusions are wrong or that more studies are needed.

3.   How strong is the evidence overall?

Understand how this information fits in with other evidence. Some sources generally strive to provide unbiased coverage, while others may be intentionally biased. Consider how many sides of the story you hear, whether your source tells you about all of the possibilities, and the weight of the evidence.

Remember that extensive coverage of a story can be misleading if it does not reflect the amount of evidence that supports the claim. In particular, the results of early studies can turn out to be right or wrong after time. Americans have mistakenly rejected results that later proved true, and accepted results that later proved false.

4.   Does this information matter?

Determine whether the information changes your thinking and leads you to respond. Just because information appears in the media does not mean that it affects you or someone you care about. Some risks (like accidents and homicide) may be overreported in the news media, while other, less newsworthy risks (like heart disease and stroke) may be underreported. The result is that you might be led to worry about small risks that appear to be big and to ignore big risks that appear to be small.

5.   What do the numbers mean?

Remember that understanding the importance of a risk requires understanding the numbers. Information about health risks gives the chances of an outcome occurring. To avoid confusion, put the numbers into a format that you can understand. Remember that you can also write 1 in 100 as 1%, ten thousand out of a million, 0.01, 1×10^{-2}, one penny out of a dollar, or 10 in 1,000.

Researchers report their findings as expected values within a range. The breadth of the range shows how confident they are about the results. When only one number is reported, it is probably pulled out of a range and it does not inform you about the researcher's confidence in the result. In such cases, it is important to understand whether the number reflects the worst case, the best case, or something in the middle.

Remember that risks change with time, and that some people will have higher or lower risk numbers than other people. Think about any habits or behaviors you have that put you at a higher or lower risk for a particular outcome.

6.   How does this risk compare to others?

Put the risk into context. One important skill for comparing risks is making sure that comparisons all involve the chances of the same outcome, like death. For example, the following numbers of U.S. deaths per year per 10 million people all compare deaths per year:
- 200,000 from heart disease (people over 64)
- 6,000 from lung cancer
- 3,000 from accidents
- 1,000 from homicides
- 400 from accidental poisoning
- 20 from train accidents
- 2 from lightning

Since numbers about risk can be presented in many forms (like the chances of dying from a cause over a lifetime, during a year, or during an event), make sure you compare similar forms. Consider that reporting different parts of a range for different risks (the best case for one vs. the worst case for another) can be very misleading.

Finally, in making comparisons, other factors may be important to you. For example, consider the extent to which you
- Think the risk is new
- Choose the risk
- Can control, manage, or prevent harm
- Gain things you want by accepting the risk
- Fear the risk
- Feel anxious from lack of knowledge

These factors might mislead you sometimes. For example, an unfamiliar chemical like dihydrogen monoxide might sound threatening, even though it is simply another name for water.

Remember that science can not answer the question "Is it safe?" for anyone. You must decide what is an acceptable risk and make health decisions based on your personal judgment.

7.   What actions can be taken to reduce risk?

Identify the ways that you can improve your health. Be creative. Think about actions that can reduce your risk. For risks that are new to you, take the time to think about them before forming an opinion. Keep in mind that just because someone you know picks one action does not mean that the same action will be right for you.

8.   What are the trade-offs?

Make sure you can live with the trade-offs associated with different actions. Every decision involves trade-offs. When talking about medications, trade-offs are often called side effects, like when the medicine you take to get rid of your headache upsets your stomach. Ignoring potential trade-offs when considering an action to reduce or eliminate a risk might ultimately put you (or someone else) at greater risk.

Taking action can also lead to trade-offs of other important resources, particularly time and money. Some people object to the idea that they might be asked to trade between health and money or other factors. Most people make these choices automatically, however, by driving slower at the cost of a few extra minutes or spending money to buy a bicycle helmet for their child or a smoke detector for their home. Remember that resources spent to reduce one type of risk are not available for other activities.

9.   What else do I need to know?

Focus on identifying the information that would help you make a better decision. Remember that scientific information is always somewhat uncertain even if it is not reported that way. Think about what information is missing and how you would use more information if you had it. Keep in mind that if you rely on the headlines as a basis for managing your health, you are likely to overlook the well-established (and consequently not newsworthy) strategies for improving your health.

10. Where can I get more information?
Find the information that you want. Try:
- Your health care provider
- Manufacturers and manuals or labels that come with their products (my recommendation is that you actually take the time to read these!)
- Libraries
- Your original source
- Your local Department of Health
- Government agencies (many linked from www.consumer.gov)
    Consumer Product Safety Commission (www.cpsc.gov)
    Department of Agriculture (www.usda.gov)
    Department of Health and Human Services (www.dhs.gov)
        Centers for Disease Control and Prevention (www.cdc.gov)
        Food and Drug Administration (www.fda.gov)
        National Institutes of Health (www.nih.gov)
    Department of Transportation (www.dot.gov)
    Environmental Protection Agency (www.epa.gov)
    Occupational Safety and Health Administration (www.osha.gov)
- Consumer groups
- The Internet.

You can find these 10 questions and links to some helpful Internet sites at the www.aorm.com web site. Remember, when it comes to using the Internet, no quality control exists. Buyer (and user) beware....

A March 1996 pamphlet from the Federal Trade Commission (FTC) Bureau of Consumer Protection called *Fraudulent Health Claims: Don't Be Fooled* identified the following as "typical phrases and marketing techniques used to deceive consumers:
" • The product is advertised as a quick and effective cure-all for a wide range of ailments or for an undiagnosed pain.
" • The promoters use key words, such as *scientific breakthrough, miraculous cure, exclusive product, secret ingredient* or *ancient remedy*.
" • The promoter claims the medical profession or research scientists have conspired to suppress the product.
" • The advertisement includes undocumented case histories claiming amazing results.
" • The product is advertised as available from only one source, and payment in advance is required."
The FTC also suggests that the first rule of thumb for evaluating health claims is "be skeptical. If it sounds too good to be true, it probably is." Consumers should not rely on promises of money-back guarantees, since some sellers may not stay around long enough to respond to their requests. Also, remember that the Dietary Supplement Health and Education Act of 1994 restricted the legal authority of the Food and Drug Administration (FDA) so that it *can not* legally require companies that market dietary supplements and ethnic remedies to prove the safety and effectiveness of their products nor can it enforce standards for product quality. This contrasts with pharmaceutical products that must go through a strict FDA approval process for demonstrating their safety and efficacy *before* they enter the market.

How This Book Can Help

This book follows a very simple structure with each chapter focused on a theme related to risk. The beginning of each chapter provides a short introduction and list of quotes, because as Plato said, "The beginning is the most important part of the work." A series of cartoons follows the quotes. In a few cases, I made notes on the cartoon pages to help provide some context that may be unfamiliar to some readers.

The rest of this introduction includes a brief overview of the chapter themes with one quote and cartoon introducing each theme. Chapters 1-5 relate mainly to risk assessment; chapters 6-8 relate mainly to risk management; chapter 9 covers risk communication; and chapters 10, 11, and 12 address law and policy, health care in the U.S., and signs of the times, respectively.

An epilogue gives closing thoughts. For those who might come to rely on this book as a resource, the index for the quotes and the index for the cartoon artists begin on pages 297 and 305, respectively. I also included in the **Extras** that start on page 307 some excellent Guidelines for Communicating Uncertain Science on Nutrition, Food Safety, and Health developed for all parties involved in the communication process (particularly scientists, journalists, journal editors, industry, consumers, and other interest groups). Students of my course will recognize this as an assigned reading. Following these Guidelines, the **Extras** section provides some exercises for those motivated readers to gain some new insights and test their risk detective skills (also known as class exercises to my students) and it provides a list of some of the quotes that I collected and intended to use in this book, but that I debunked or could not verify or properly attribute. If you can verify any of the quotes in the **Extras** or if you find any errors in this book, then please let me know because I will post corrections at www.aorm.com.

Not surprisingly, what you take from this book depends entirely on you. It might simply offer a few laughs or a useful quote, or it could change the way that you think about life's risks. I hope that readers will find useful fodder for discussions related to risk in these materials. For example, if you browse through this book in your doctor's office, you might find just the cartoon you need to help start a discussion on a topic that you need to talk about but can't seem to find the words to start. Alternatively, perhaps one of the quotes will help you to bridge a divide between colleagues that encourages improved collaboration or help you make a connection with a family member to bring insight or humor into a discussion about a risk.

"`Would you tell me, please, which way I ought to go from here?'
`That depends a good deal on where you want to get to,' said the Cat.
`I don't much care where--' said Alice.
`Then it doesn't matter which way you go,' said the Cat.
`--so long as I get SOMEWHERE,' Alice added as an explanation.
`Oh, you're sure to do that,' said the Cat, `if you only walk long enough.'" *Lewis Carroll*

Chapter 1 focuses on **science and technology**. Science and technology form the foundation for risk analysis. They serve as the sources of our evidence about life's risks and the solutions we can use to deal with them. The number of quotes and cartoons about science and technology baffles the mind, although they represent only a very tiny fraction of the huge, ever-growing, amazing body of available information. I found it very hard to choose the set to include in this book, and even harder still to select just one of each for this page.

"No idea is so antiquated that it was not once modern. No idea is so modern that it will not someday be antiquated." *Ellen Glasgow*

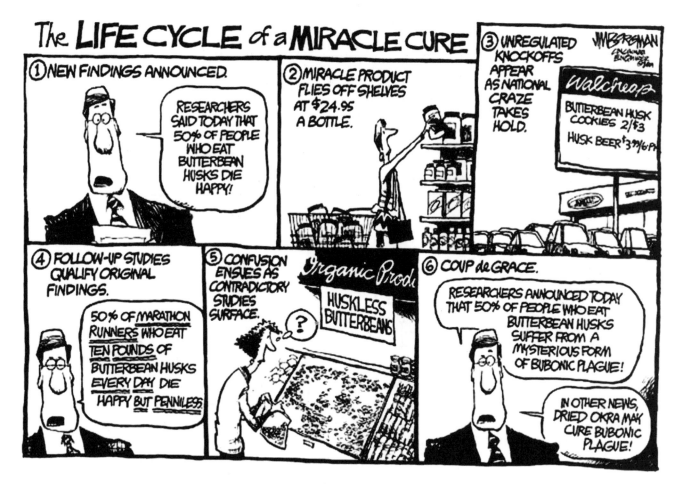

© 5/18/01 Jim Borgman, Cincinnati Enquirer. Reprinted with special permission of King Features Syndicate.

Chapter 2 looks at how **it's all in the numbers**. Since risk analysts rely on mathematical models to characterize risks, this chapter takes on math, modeling, and numbers. While no knowledge of mathematics is required to enjoy this chapter, I hope that this chapter helps motivate the significant improvements in numeracy education now required to provide everyone with the basic tools they need to understand risk estimates. I believe that risk education and training in probability and statistics need to start early in life, and we need to appreciate that it's never too early to learn to make good choices!

"All models are wrong but some are useful." *George Box*

Chapter 3 focuses on the concept of **variability**, which simply means that things can be different in real and important ways. For example, people come in different shapes, sizes, ages, genders, genetic compositions, and so on. These real differences do not go away simply because we get better information about the people. Variability explains why "one size fits all" can only be considered an enormous oversimplification.

"The difference between the *almost*-right word and the *right* word is really a large matter - it's the difference between the lightning bug and the lightning." *Mark Twain*

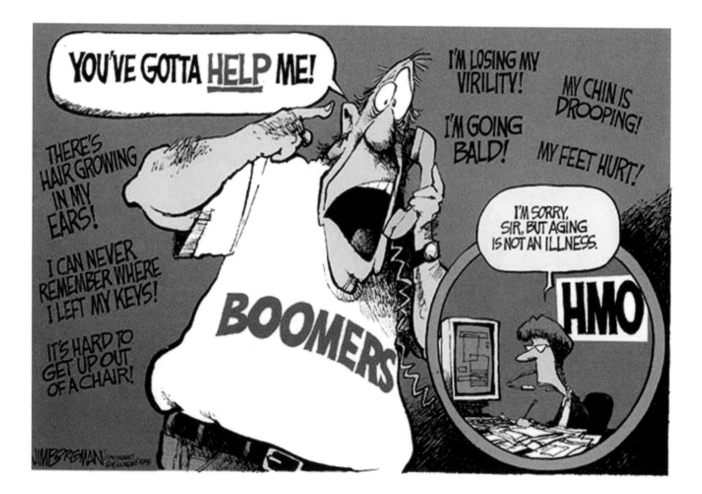

© 7/19/98 Jim Borgman, Cincinnati Enquirer. Reprinted with special permission of King Features Syndicate.

Chapter 4 covers **uncertainty**, which differs distinctly from variability. Uncertainty refers to a lack of perfect knowledge. Uncertainty can keep people up at night with the "if I only knew" blues as they agonize over the possibilities. Fortunately, in some cases uncertainty may be reduced by obtaining better information. Uncertainty tends to be annoying, but it can become remarkably empowering once one comes to terms with it.

"If a man will begin with certainties, he shall end in doubts; but if he will be content to begin with doubts, he shall end in certainties." *Francis Bacon*

"Before we can prepare for Y2K, we have to determine the severity of the problem. Heads, it will be a minor nuisance. Tails, it will be the end of civilization as we know it."

Y2K stands for the year 2000, when all of the computer systems were supposed to fail and shut down the world, but you can substitute in any current Doomsday prophecy....

Chapter 5 focuses on **errors**, something that we all worry about and deal with. Errors come from honest mistakes, misunderstandings, carelessness, bad choices, system failures, and various other sources. Errors provide the most potent lessons learned, and typically the magnitude of the value of the lesson relates directly to the consequences of the error.

"There is the greatest practical benefit in making a few failures early in life." *Thomas Henry Huxley*

Chapter 6 introduces **choices and risk trade-offs**. The chapter emphasizes the need to think about risks in context.

"False is the idea of utility that sacrifices a thousand real advantages for one imaginary or trifling inconvenience; that would take fire from men because it burns, and water because one may drown in it; that has no remedy for evils, except destruction." *Cesare Beccaria*

Chapter 7 looks at **effectiveness, benefits, and costs**, with the clear perspective that these represent critically important considerations when you make choices. A simple look at the pros and cons of the options and how well they work may suffice for some decisions, but one should never skip the step of pondering the many attributes of decisions.

"The first and most imperative necessity in war is money, for money means everything else - men, guns, ammunition." *Ida M. Tarbell*

Chapter 8 addresses **values and preferences**, which determine how we evaluate options available to us and select the best. These turn out to be critically important to understand, although sometimes unstable and nearly impossible to measure.

"I know of no safe depository of the ultimate powers of the society but the people themselves; and if we think them not enlightened enough to exercise their control with a wholesome discretion, the remedy is not to take it from them, but to inform their discretion." *Thomas Jefferson*

"O.K., who *can* put a price on love? Jim?"

Chapter 9 focuses on **risks in the media**, including strategies used for risk communication. The news and entertainment media demand so much time and attention and they provide so many messages about risk every day that we have reached a point where everyone needs basic training in media deconstruction. This chapter will get you started.

"Ignorant free speech often works against the speaker. That is one of several reasons why it must be given rein instead of suppressed." *Anna Quindlen*

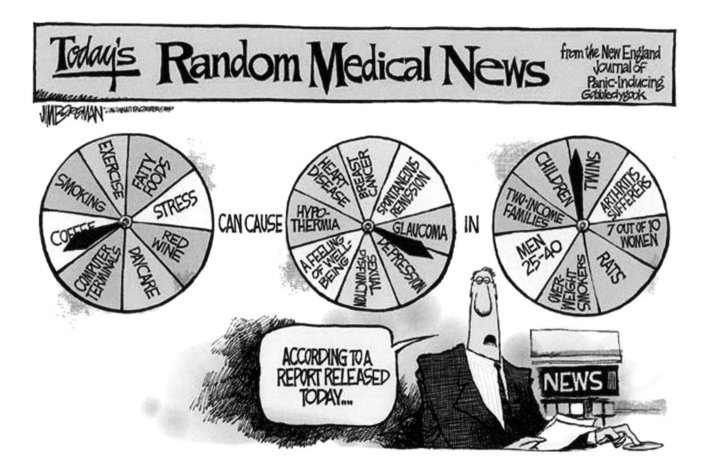

© 4/27/97 Jim Borgman, Cincinnati Enquirer. Reprinted with special permission of King Features Syndicate.

In Chapter 10 **risks meet law and policy**. The law frames much of the way that we regulate risks, and this book would be incomplete without this chapter. As much as people like to hate and joke about lawyers, we must all remember that they often make the rules. This is a must-read for lawyers and policy makers and for those who work with them.

"The first thing we do, let's kill all the lawyers." *William Shakespeare*

Chapter 11 takes on the current **health care in the U.S.** Given the absence of universal health care coverage, readers outside the U.S. may experience some difficulty relating to some parts of this chapter. Suffice it to say that our for-profit insurance, pharmaceutical, and health provider industries generate a lot of funny material. This chapter provides insight about how the system is working (or not), and the patient's role in navigating the system and pursuing good health.

"It may seem a strange principle to enunciate as the very first requirement in a Hospital that it should do the sick no harm." *Florence Nightingale*

"We're running a little behind, so I'd like each of you to ask yourself, 'Am I really that sick, or would I just be wasting the doctor's valuable time?'"

Chapter 12 focuses on the **signs of the times**. This last chapter takes a final look at the current times, with a glance toward the future and some challenges to current ways of thinking.

"Wahoo! Take chances, make mistakes, get messy!" *Joanna Cole and Bruce Degen*

-1-
Science and Technology

As a child I wanted to know everything about everything and to understand how things work. Some things never change. Science still fascinates me, and scientists are some of my favorite people. I think of science in simplest terms as knowledge and the process of acquiring knowledge. Science promotes understanding and reduces ignorance. In my view, the best scientists can provide context and effectively communicate about their work.

In contrast, I think of technology as the application of knowledge, typically to achieve an objective. For example, technology translates knowledge about fuels into means to harness them and to use them to power engines that transport, heat, refrigerate, and manufacture. Technology provides food in sufficient quantities to feed a growing population of billions, health care to help people live longer and better lives, and tools to send information around the world.

With science and technology serving as the subjects of so many books and playing critical roles in our everyday lives, they represent obvious foundations of risk analysis. Scientists and engineers always play important roles in society, not only as explorers and enablers, but also as teachers. They challenge the uninformed and ignorant. No matter what you do, what choices you make, or whether you like science or not, you must realize that our society relies on science and technology to detect, measure, manage, and convey information about risks. We must invest in basic scientific training for all and continue to appreciate the contributions of those who acquire knowledge that improves human lives and our world.

***

"I do not feel obliged to believe that the same God who has endowed us with senses, reason, and intellect has intended us to forego their use and by some other means to give us knowledge which we can attain by them." *Galileo Galilei*

"The method of scientific investigation is nothing but the expression of the necessary mode of working of the human mind." *Thomas Henry Huxley*

"Some of these questions don't have finite answers, but the questions themselves are important. Don't stop asking, and don't let anybody tell you the questions aren't worth it. They are." *Madeline L'Engle*

"[Scientists] regard it as a major intellectual virtue, to know what not to think about." *C.P. Snow*

"After all, the ultimate goal of all research is not objectivity, but truth." *Helene Deutsch*

"Science, after all, is only an expression for our ignorance of our own ignorance." *Samuel Butler*

"I do not know what I may appear to the world; but to myself I seem to have been only like a boy playing on the seashore, and diverting myself in now and then finding a smoother pebble or a prettier shell than ordinary, whilst the great ocean of truth lay all undiscovered before me."
Sir Isaac Newton

"The negative cautions of science are never popular." *Margaret Mead*

"An important scientific innovation rarely makes its way by gradually winning over and converting its opponents…. What does happen is that its opponents gradually die out and that the growing generation is familiarized with the idea from the beginning." *Max Planck*

"Life in a settlement does several things to you. Among others, it teaches you that education and culture have little to do with real wisdom, the wisdom that comes from life experiences."
Alice Hamilton

"The aim of science is, on the one hand, as complete a comprehension as possible of the connection between perceptible experiences in their totality, and, on the other hand, the achievement of this aim by employing a minimum of primary concepts and relations."
Albert Einstein

"It is the lone worker who makes the first advance in a subject: the details may be worked out by a team, but the prime idea is due to the enterprise, thought and perception of an individual."
Sir Alexander Fleming

"Science is the search for truth - it is not a game in which one tries to beat his opponent, to do harm to others." *Linus Carl Pauling*

"… one of the excellent virtues of our true scientists is that they never hesitate to own themselves in the wrong by a complete reversal of old teaching by new." *Mary D. Chambers*

"So long as the mother, Ignorance, lives, it is not safe for Science, the offspring, to divulge the hidden causes of things." *Johannes Kepler*

"Science is a systematic study of facts. It must be distinguished both from philosophy and from everyday consciousness. From the latter it differs only in method, for both science and the every-day consciousness have to do with phenomena or facts; but science studies these phenomena critically, analyzes them into their ultimate parts, and classifies them by their most essential likenesses, whereas the everyday conscious observes facts uncritically, as conglomerates, with little or no analysis and with only superficial recognition of the most striking likenesses." *Mary Whiton Calkins*

"If you wish to make an apple pie from scratch, you must first invent the universe." *Carl Sagan*

"If an idea, I reasoned, were really a valuable one, there must be a way of realizing it." *Elizabeth Blackwell*

"Knowledge is power." *Francis Bacon*

"I worry about scientists discovering that lettuce has been fattening all along...." *Erma Bombeck*

"...that is what learning is. You suddenly understand something you've understood all your life, but in a new way." *Doris Lessing*

"Scientific knowledge is a body of statements of varying degrees of certainty - some most unsure, some nearly sure, none *absolutely* certain." *Richard P. Feynman*

"All my life through, the new sights of Nature made me rejoice like a child." *Marie Curie*

"No endeavor that is worthwhile is simple in prospect; if it is right, it will be simple in retrospect." *Edward Teller*

"To work in the service of life and the living
 In search of the answers to questions unknown" *John Denver*

"Theories that go counter to the facts of human nature are foredoomed." *Edith Hamilton*

"Inanimate objects are classified scientifically into three major categories - those that don't work, those that break down and those that get lost." *Russell Baker*

"One never goes so far as when one doesn't know where one is going." *Johann Wolfgang von Goethe*

"Sunrises and sunsets are spectacular from orbit." *Sally Ride*

"The truth is rarely pure and never simple." *Oscar Wilde*

"Civilization as it is known today could not have evolved, nor can it survive, without an adequate food supply. Yet food is something that is taken for granted by most world leaders despite the fact that more than half of the population of the world is hungry. Man seems to insist on ignoring the lessons available from history." *Norman Borlaug*

"The greatest invention of the nineteenth century was the invention of the method of invention." *A.N. Whitehead*

"It is my hope that all children, boys and girls, will see this mission and be inspired to reach for their dreams, because dreams do come true." *Lt. Col. Eileen M. Collins*

"...to explore strange new worlds ...to seek out new life and new civilizations ...to boldly go where no man has gone before." *Gene Roddenberry*

Welcome to the Age of Risk Management. Please keep in mind that miracles, discoveries, and ignorance will continue.... Enjoy! *K.M.T.*

"TODAY'S PROBLEMS SHOULD HAVE BEEN SOLVED IN THE 1950s, BUT IN THE '50s WE WERE SOLVING THE PROBLEMS OF THE '20s, AND IN THE '20s WE WERE SOLVING THE PROBLEMS OF THE 1890s."

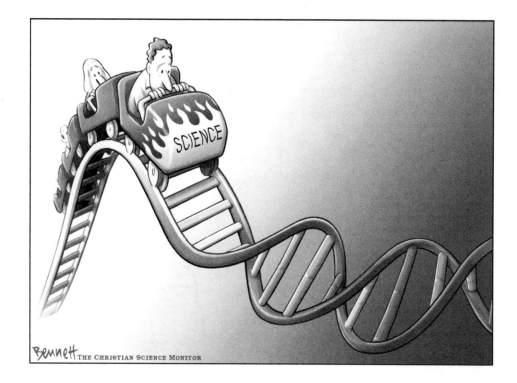

Clay Bennett 2001 © The Christian Science Monitor.

CONTROL GROUP   OUT OF CONTROL GROUP.

"UNFORTUNATELY THIS LAB IS FUNDED ONLY BY AS MUCH GOLD AS WE CAN MAKE FROM LEAD."

"I don't care what they let you do in that other lab,
you can't smoke in here."

"Some genetic engineers we turned out to be!"

"YES, I'D LIKE TO ORDER ITEM NUMBER 94773-B, THE DO-IT-YOURSELF CHROMOSOME MANIPULATION MAKEOVER KIT WITH THE CLONING ADAPTOR....OH, AND, WHAT THE HECK, A SET OF FROZEN IDENTICAL TWINS, IN BLONDE."

"MAN, I'D LIKE TO OWN THE PATENT ON THAT GENETIC SEQUENCE!"

"BIGGEST DAMN VIRUS I'VE EVER SEEN!"

I dedicate this page to the amazing team of people working at the time of publishing to eradicate polio, to their predecessors, including those who eradicated smallpox, and to those who will follow. Let us all hope that vaccines will continue to be powerful weapons of mass salvation, and that humans will continue to use scientific knowledge and technological tools to lengthen and improve lives. *K.M.T.*

"AS I MENTIONED NEXT WEEK IN MY TALK ON REVERSIBLE TIME..."

"AS YOU KNOW, WE PUT SARDINE GENES IN POTATOES, AND POTATO GENES IN SARDINES. THE RESULTS ARE IN. WE WON'T DO ANYTHING LIKE THAT AGAIN."

"IT STARTED WITH A SIMPLE CASE OF PEER-REVIEW."

"WE COLLABORATE. I'M AN EXPERT, BUT NOT AN AUTHORITY, AND DR. GELBIS IS AN AUTHORITY, BUT NOT AN EXPERT."

© 8/26/01 Jim Borgman, Cincinnati Enquirer. Reprinted with special permission of King Features Syndicate.

© 5/20/01 Jim Borgman, Cincinnati Enquirer. Reprinted with special permission of King Features Syndicate.

" I AM NOW AVAILABLE BY PHONE, FAX, E-MAIL, SNAIL MAIL, VOICE MAIL, OVERNIGHT DELIVERY, CAR PHONE, CELL PHONE AND PAGER............HIDE ME. "

© 1/29/01 Jim Borgman, Cincinnati Enquirer. Reprinted with special permission of King Features Syndicate.

"OF COURSE IT WON'T TOAST YOUR BAGEL, SILLY... YOU FORGOT TO ENTER THE 18-DIGIT-ELECTRIC-POWER-SERVICE-PROVIDER ACCESS CODE FOLLOWED BY OUR FAMILY PERSONAL IDENTIFICATION NUMBER."

© 5/14/97 Jim Borgman, Cincinnati Enquirer. Reprinted with special permission of King Features Syndicate.

Dedicated to those who staff information technology departments everywhere. *K.M.T.*

-2-
It's All in the Numbers

Numeracy represents a critical skill, and one that remains remarkably underappreciated by many people in today's society. Studies continue to show surprising results when it comes to how well people understand numbers. Consider the following results from a study that asked 500 women from a health registry to answer the following questions:
"1. Imagine that we flip a fair coin 1,000 times. What is your best guess about how many times the coin would come up heads in 1,000 flips? _____ times out of 1,000."
"2. In the BIG BUCKS LOTTERY, the chance of winning a $10 prize is 1%. What is your best guess about how many people would win a $10 prize if 1,000 people each buy a single ticket to BIG BUCKS? _____ times out of 1,000."
"3. In ACME PUBLISHING SWEEPSTAKES, the chance of winning a car is 1 in 1,000. What percent of tickets to ACME PUBLISHING SWEEPSTAKES win a car? _____ %"
"Thirty percent of respondents had 0 correct answers, 28% had 1 correct answer, 26% had 2 correct answers, and 16% had 3 correct answers." *Lisa Schwartz et al.*

Risk analysis depends on mathematics as its primary language. Risk assessors translate science into models of the world. They use probability (the mathematics of characterizing chance), and statistics (the mathematics of synthesizing and interpretating numerical data). They rely on models and measurements, and they make assumptions in an effort to manage the complexity of the problem. While you don't need to understand calculus and differential equations to understand the concepts of risk, some basic numeracy skills are required. You need to understand the many ways we represent numbers and their interpretation. You should recognize that differences in the number of significant figures (for example between 1.001 and 1.0 and 1) means something. Numbers can represent highly precise quantities (meaning well-defined and well-measured) or very imprecise quantities. Numerical estimates may also vary in their accuracy (meaning their ability to represent the true value). You should also feel comfortable with scientific notation and recognize that 1×10^{-3} is the same as 1 in 1,000 or 0.1% (the answer to question 3 above).

Once you appreciate the basics, you should also realize that risks get reported with a wide range of metrics. These include individual risks (for example referring to your personal chance of getting cancer over some period of time) and population risks (for example referring to the expected number of cancer cases in a group of individuals over some time period). They might also represent absolute risks that tell you the probability overall, or relative risks that tell you how two risks compare without providing context about the baseline. Remember that your perception can also depend on whether the information is presented as positive (half-full) or negative (half-empty). Flipping the statements and looking for alternative ways to state them might change your perception. For example, if you hear about a small number of people affected, remember that this means a large number are not affected, and vice versa.

"Philosophy is written in this grand book-I mean the universe-which stands continually open to our gaze, but it cannot be understood unless one first learns to comprehend the language and interpret the characters in which it is written. It is written in the language of mathematics, and its characters are triangles, circles, and other geometrical figures, without which it is humanly impossible to understand a single word of it." *Galileo Galilei*

"When you can measure what you are speaking about, and express it in numbers, you know something about it; but when you cannot measure it, when you cannot express it in numbers, your knowledge is of a meager and unsatisfactory kind: it may be the beginning of knowledge, but you have scarcely, in your thoughts, advanced to the stage of science." *William Thomson, Lord Kelvin*

"For at least 2,000,000 years, men have been reproducing and multiplying on a little automated space ship called Earth." *Richard Buckminster Fuller*

"What is man in nature? Nothing in relation to the infinite, everything in relation to nothing, a mean between nothing and everything." *Blaise Pascal*

"In order to talk about the nature of the universe and to discuss questions such as whether it has a beginning or an end, you have to be clear about what a scientific theory is. I shall take the simple-minded view that a theory is just a model of the universe, or a restricted part of it, and a set of rules that relate quantities in the model to observations that we make. It exists in our minds and does not have any other reality (whatever that means)." *Stephen W. Hawking*

"All the mathematical sciences are founded on relations between physical laws and laws of numbers, so that the aim of exact science is to reduce the problems of nature to the determination of quantities by operations with numbers." *James Clerk Maxwell*

"The theory of probability is at the bottom nothing but common sense reduced to calculus." *Pierre de Laplace*

"Mathematics takes us still further from what is human, into the region of absolute necessity, to which not only the actual world, but every possible world, must conform." *Bertrand Russell*

"Perhaps even a perfectly reasonable boundary value problem does not have a solution." *Cathleen Synge Morawetz*

"Genius is one percent inspiration and ninety-nine percent perspiration." *Thomas Edison*

"It appears that there are enormous differences of opinion as to the probability of a failure with loss of vehicle and of human life. The estimates range from roughly 1 in 100 to 1 in 100,000. The higher frequency comes from working engineers, and the very low figures from management. What are the causes and consequences of this lack of agreement?" *Richard P. Feynman*

"Round numbers are always false." *Samuel Johnson*

"The believer in the law of small numbers practices science as follows.... He gambles his research hypothesis on small samples without realizing that the odds against him are unreasonably high. He overestimates power.... He has undue confidence in early trends... and in the stability of observed patterns. He overestimates significance.... He rarely attributes deviation of results from expectations to sampling variability, because he finds a causal 'explanation' for any discrepancy." *Amos Tversky and Daniel Kahneman*

"The statistical correlation of two variables does not *ipso facto* signify that either one is the cause or effect of the other." *John Punnett Peters*

"The systematic approach of decision analysis has its merits and demerits, and vivid testimony appears on both sides of the ledger. Also, what is a merit to some is a demerit to others." *Howard Raiffa*

"In the long run, we are all dead." *John Maynard Keynes*

"Whether or not they realize it and whether or not they take explicit account of the varying degree of risk involved, individuals choosing among occupations, securities, or lines of business activity are making choices analogous to those that they make when they decide whether to buy insurance or to gamble." *Milton Friedman and L. J. Savage*

"Anyone who considers arithmetical methods of producing random digits is, of course, in a state of sin." *John von Neumann*

"I certainly feel that the time is not far distant when a knowledge of the principle of diet will be an essential part of one's education. Then mankind will eat to live, be able to do better mental and physical work, and disease will be less frequent." *Fannie Farmer*

"The most important maxim for data analysis to heed, and one which many statisticians seem to have shunned, is this: 'Far better an approximate answer to the *right* question, which is often vague, than an *exact* answer to the wrong question, which can always be made precise.'" *John W. Tukey*

"The time when speculative theory and observational research may profitably go hand-in-hand is when the possibilities, or at any rate the probabilities, can be narrowed down by experiment, and the theory can indicate the tests by which the remaining wrong paths can be blocked up one by one." *Sir Arthur Stanley Eddington*

"(Statistics is) the most important science in the whole world: for upon it depends the practical application of every other & of every Art: the one science essential to all Political & Social Administration all Education & Organization based on experience, for it only gives results of our experience." *Florence Nightingale*

"Though analogy is often misleading, it is the least misleading thing we have." *Samuel Butler*

Always check the units of all equations, and then check them again. *K.M.T.*

"BUT THIS IS THE SIMPLIFIED VERSION FOR THE GENERAL PUBLIC."

"And this is Fred, our senior Risk Assessment Manager. He sees around corners most of us don't even know are there!"

HOW GASOLINE PRICES ARE DETERMINED

"A billion is a thousand million? Why wasn't I informed of this?"

Copyright 2003 by Randy Glasbergen.
www.glasbergen.com

**"We've devised a new security encryption code.
Each digit is printed upside down."**

© 1999 Randy Glasbergen.

**"I'm paid $4,000,000 a year. You're paid $40,000.
The only difference is a few zeros. Everyone knows
that zero equals nothing. So what's the problem?"**

It's All in the Numbers   65

"Your insurance only pays 80% of my fee,
so I only took out 80% of your appendix."

"Unless we receive the outstanding balance within
ten days, we will have no choice but to destroy your
credit rating, ruin your reputation, and make you wish
you were never born. If you have already sent the
seven cents, please disregard this notice."

"Oh, if only it were so simple."

It's All in the Numbers

© 4/16/00 Jim Borgman, Cincinnati Enquirer. Reprinted with special permission of King Features Syndicate.

"FEWER THAN ONE IN TEN THOUSAND — SOMETHING LIKE ONE IN FOURTEEN THOUSAND — GETS THESE SIDE EFFECTS. HARDLY ANYBODY GETS THESE SIDE EFFECTS. THEY'RE EXTREMELY RARE. YOU SHOULD BE VERY PROUD."

-3-
Variability

If variety is the spice of life, then variability characterizes the spiciness. Variability refers to the real differences and similarities that exist between and within people, places, and things both in space and over time. You see variability all around you all the time. People come in different ages, shapes, colors, and sizes. They express different preferences and operate under different constraints. Parents appreciate variability in children's preferences about favorite foods and toys, and that sometimes kids prefer no variability as they request the same food repeatedly.

When scientists make observations they characterize variability using numbers. While we look for general rules that apply all of the time, in reality we rely on rules that apply most or even some of the time. In the context of risk managment, variability means that the best choice for some may not represent the best choice for others. This means risk assessors must model variability to figure out when it matters. Although the media often report scientific data without reporting on variaibilty in the observations, variability that should be communicated often exists.

***

"We haven't all had the good fortune to be ladies; we haven't all been generals, or poets, or statesmen; but when the toast works down to the babies, we stand on common ground." *Mark Twain*

"Minds ripen at very different ages." *Elizabeth Montagu*

"I've been rich and I've been poor. Believe me honey, rich is better." *Sophie Tucker*

"The optimist was the man who did not mind what happened, so long as it did not happen to him. The pessimist was the man who lived with the optimist." *Sir Winston Churchill*

"Perhaps our national ambition to standardize ourselves has behind it the notion that democracy means standardization. But standardization is the surest way to destroy the initiative, to benumb the creative impulse above all else essential to the vitality and growth of democratic ideals." *Ida M. Tarbell*

"[An] average result is not to be taken as the positive and absolute expression of the law before us. The result is still subject to a certain degree of variableness... the amount of which can be ascertained... by the calculation of probabilities." *Elisha Bartlett*

"Beauty is in the eye of the beholder." *Margaret Wolfe Hungerford*

"It's pretty hard to retain the characteristics of one's sex after a certain age." *Colette*

"Uncertainty and variability have fundamentally different ramifications for science and judgment: uncertainty forces decision-makers to judge how *probable* it is that risks will be overestimated or underestimated for every member of the exposed population, whereas variability forces them to cope with the *certainty* that different individuals will be subjected to risks both above and below any reference point one chooses." *National Research Council*

"I have called this principle, by which each slight variation, if useful, is preserved, by the term Natural Selection." *Charles Darwin*

"... no circumstance in the natural world is more inexplicable than the diversity of form and colour in the human race." *Mary Somerville*

"The joy of life is variety; the tenderest love requires to be renewed by intervals of absence." *Samuel Johnson*

"The more education a woman has, the wider the gap between men's and women's earnings for the same work." *Sandra Day O'Connor*

"In a hierarchy, every employee tends to rise to his level of incompetence." *Laurence J. Peter*

"No animal is so inexhaustible as an excited infant." *Amy Leslie*

"The average family exists only on paper and its average budget is fiction, invented by statisticians for the convenience of statisticians." *Sylvia Porter*

"At no point in my life have I ever felt as though I were an American." *Toni Morrison*

"Mind and spirit together make up that which separates us from the rest of the animal world, that which enables a man to know the truth and that which enables him to die for the truth." *Edith Hamilton*

"Variability is the law of life, and as no two faces are the same, so no two bodies are alike, and no two individuals react alike under the abnormal conditions which we know as disease." *William Osler*

"Although we had no money I was rich as I could be
in my coat of many colors my Momma made for me." *Dolly Parton*

"There are no little events in life, those we think of no consequence may be full of fate, and it is at our own risk if we neglect the acquaintances and opportunities that seem to be casually offered, and of small importance." *Amelia E. Barr*

"The existence of a majority logically implies a corresponding minority." *Philip K. Dick*

One size never fits all. *K.M.T.*

"IT APPEARS YOU'RE A BIT OVERQUALIFIED TO BE EXPLOITED, BUT SOMEWHAT UNDERQUALIFIED TO EXPLOIT OTHERS."

" I TRUST YOUR GENETIC CODE IS IN ORDER ?"

"WE COULDN'T CONNECT. HE KEPT SPOUTING TECHNOBABBLE, AND I, OF COURSE, KEPT COMING BACK WITH PSYCHOBABBLE."

© 4/28/99 Jim Borgman, Cincinnati Enquirer. Reprinted with special permission of King Features Syndicate.

"Yes, I realize that we are free agents, but I have to take on the additional risk of pregnancy and am more susceptible to certain sexually transmitted diseases, so I think you should pay for the movie."

"Never, ever, think outside the box."

Risk in Perspective

Variability   81

-4-
Uncertainty

Uncertainty comes from lack of perfect knowledge. It refers to all unknowns at any point in time. Risk analysts use probabilities to characterize uncertainty. It's part of life, and it makes life interesting.

***

"Certainty generally is illusion, and repose is not the destiny of man." *Oliver Wendell Holmes, Jr.*

"I was gratified to be able to answer promptly, and I did. I said I didn't know." *Mark Twain*

"A statistical analysis, properly conducted, is a delicate dissection of uncertainties, a surgery of suppositions." *M.J. Moroney*

"Isn't it splendid to think of all the things there are to find out about? It makes me feel glad to be alive - it's such an interesting world. It wouldn't be half so interesting if we knew all about everything, would it? There'd be no scope for imagination then, would there?" *Lucy Montgomery*

"You can use probabilities in direct proportion to your ignorance of the uniqueness of the individual." *Lawrence L. Weed*

"There is no certainty where one can neither apply any of the mathematical sciences nor any of those which are based upon the mathematical sciences." *Leonardo da Vinci*

"It is only by risking our persons from one hour to another that we live at all. And often enough our faith beforehand in an uncertified result is the only thing that makes the result come true." *William James*

"The first is the matter of judging evidence-well, the first thing really is, before you begin you must not know the answer. So you begin by being uncertain as to what the answer is. This is very, very important…. The question of doubt and uncertainty is what is necessary to begin; for if you already know the answer there is no need to gather any evidence about it." *Richard P. Feynman*

"A doctor must accept and live with uncertainty and fallibility, inescapable parts of any walk of life but harder to bear in matters of life or death." *Peter Richards*

"He is no wise man who will quit a certainty for an uncertainty." *Samuel Johnson*

"Life is the art of drawing sufficient conclusions from insufficient premises." *Samuel Butler*

"Security is mostly a superstition. It does not exist in nature, nor do the children of men as a whole experience it. Avoiding danger is no safer in the long run than outright exposure. Life is either a daring adventure, or nothing." *Helen Keller*

"I cannot forecast to you the action of Russia. It is a riddle wrapped in a mystery inside an enigma." *Sir Winston Churchill*

"Ignorance is preferable to error; and he is less remote from the truth who believes nothing, than he who believes what is wrong." *Thomas Jefferson*

"As for a future life, every man must judge for himself between conflicting vague probabilities." *Charles Darwin*

"…things are for the most part very simple in books, and in practical life very complex." *Woodrow Wilson*

"Nothing is more terrible than to see ignorance in action." *Johann Wolfgang von Goethe*

"Is life worth living? It is, so you take the risk of getting up in the morning and going through the day's work." *Walter Persegati*

"A belief which leaves no place for doubt is not a belief; it is a superstition." *José Bergamín*

"As far as the laws of mathematics refer to reality, they are not certain; and as far as they are certain, they do not refer to reality." *Albert Einstein*

"When you have eliminated the impossible, whatever remains, *however improbable*, must be the truth." *Sir Arthur Conan Doyle*

"Two roads diverged in a yellow wood,
 And sorry I could not travel both
 And be one traveler, long I stood
 And looked down one as far as I could" *Robert Frost*

"The creeks ... are an active mystery, fresh every minute. Theirs is the mystery of continuous creation and all that providence implies: the uncertainty of vision, the horror of the fixed, the dissolution of the present, the intricacy of beauty, the pressure of fecundity, the elusiveness of the free, and the flawed nature of perfection." *Annie Dillard*

"It is very useful to replace the use of judgment with knowledge, but only if the result is the use of *knowledge with judgment*." *John W. Tukey*

Life improves dramatically once one chooses to be empowered by uncertainty instead of paralyzed by it. *K.M.T.*

Garfield ®
by Jim Davis

"NOT ONLY AM I STILL UNDECIDED, BUT AT THIS POINT I CAN'T EVEN DECIDE WHAT WOULD HELP ME DECIDE."

"I GIVE UP. WHERE'S THE PATIENT?"

"GRANTED, WE HAVE TO DO THE RESEARCH. AND WE CAN DO SOME RESEARCH ON THE RESEARCH. BUT I DON'T THINK WE SHOULD GET INVOLVED IN RESEARCH ON RESEARCH ON RESEARCH."

"Scientists confirmed today that everything we know about the structure of the universe is wrongedy-wrong-wrong."

"WE'VE RUN THE WHOLE GAMUT OF TESTS ON YOU, AND YOU NOW APPEAR TO BE SUFFERING FROM OVERTESTING."

"And will you be taking part in our toxicology study tonight?"

"I CAN REFER YOU EITHER TO DR. BASINSKI, A NOTED SPECIALIST, DR. HODGE-CABOT, WHO IS A PIONEER IN THE FIELD, OR CHARLIE, A GENERIC DOCTOR WHO ALSO DOES A VERY NICE JOB."

"THERE COULD BE ANY NUMBER OF CAUSES FOR THIS CONDITION. PERHAPS HE BROKE A MIRROR, OR HE WALKED UNDER A LADDER, OR SPILLED SOME SALT..."

"I CAN'T TELL IF THE DOCTOR WROTE 'FURANOTRIN' OR 'FORUNONIL' OR 'FERNOBIL', SO I'M GIVING YOU A LITTLE OF EACH."

"WE ONLY TEST OUR DRUGS ON PLANTS, SO WE HAVE TO DO LOTS AND LOTS OF EXTRAPOLATING."

"This means something
but I can't remember what!"

"WHAT'LL IT BE — A HYPOTHETICAL MOUSE IN A THEORETICAL MAZE, A SUPPOSITIONAL GUINEA PIG TESTING A HYPOTHETICAL DRUG, OR A THEORETICAL RHESUS MONKEY WITH A SUPPOSITIONAL DISEASE?"

" 'BE CAREFUL'! ALL YOU CAN TELL ME IS 'BE CAREFUL'? "

-5-
Errors

Everyone makes mistakes. Sometimes mistakes go relatively unnoticed, and other times they carry much more significant consequences. I constantly remind students to check the units of their equations carefully to avoid calculation errors. The September 23, 1999 crash of a $125 million Mars Climate Orbiter provided the poster technology for the importance of carefully checking units throughout the engineering system. NASA lost the unmanned orbiter when it missed its planned orbit and burned up in the thin atmosphere of Mars because one engineering team used metric units and another used English units, and no one caught the error.

The concepts of uncertainty and variability play a critical role in understanding errors. Problems generally arise when the guesses aren't good enough or the guessers don't convey the potential for error. For example, one cannot possibly give a single number correct answer about the distance between the Earth and Mars at all times since both planets constantly move as they orbit around the sun. The distance varies, so the correct answer changes with time. If you don't know personally remain uncertain and make a guess with some amount of error.

***

"Those who cannot remember the past are condemned to repeat it." *George Santayana*

"An expert is a man who has made all the mistakes which can be made in a very narrow field." *Niels Bohr*

"If accidents happen and you are to blame, take steps to avoid repetition of same." *Dorothy L. Sayers*

"Make it compulsory for a doctor using a brass plate to have inscribed on it, in addition to the letters of his qualifications, the words 'Remember that I too am mortal.'" *George Bernard Shaw*

"Numerical precision is the very soul of science." *Sir D'Arcy Wentworth Thompson*

"Whenever you're wrong, admit it;
 Whenever you're right, shut up." *Ogden Nash*

"When you know you're right, you don't care what others think. You know sooner or later it will come out in the wash." *Barbara McClintock*

"O hateful Error, Melancholy's child,
 Why dost thou show to the apt thoughts of men
 The things that are not?" *William Shakespeare*

"There is indeed, a specific fault in our system of science, and in the resultant understanding of the natural world…. This fault is reductionism, the view that effective understanding of a complex system can be achieved by investigating the properties of its isolated parts." *Barry Commoner*

"The greatest blunders, like the thickest ropes, are often compounded of a multitude of strands. Take the rope apart, separate it into the small threads that compose it, and you can break them one by one. You think, 'That is all there was!' But twist them all together and you have something tremendous." *Victor Hugo*

"What a chimera then is man! What a novelty! What a monster, what a chaos, what a contradiction, what a prodigy! Judge of all things, feeble earthworm, depository of truth, a sink of uncertainty and error, the glory and shame of the universe." *Blaise Pascal*

"Man errs as long as he strives." *Johann Wolfgang von Goethe*

"For a successful technology, reality must take precedence over public relations, for nature cannot be fooled." *Richard P. Feynman*

"It is a capital mistake to theorize before one has data." *Sir Arthur Conan Doyle*

"Irrationally held truths may be more harmful than reasoned errors." *Thomas Henry Huxley*

"Experience is the name everyone gives to their mistakes." *Oscar Wilde*

"To err is human, to forgive divine." *Alexander Pope*

"An error is the more dangerous in proportion to the degree of truth which it contains." *Henri-Frédéric Amiel*

"…a long habit of not thinking a thing wrong, gives it a superficial appearance of being right, and raises at first a formidable outcry in defence of custom." *Thomas Paine*

"It is error alone which needs the support of government. Truth can stand by itself." *Thomas Jefferson*

"The study of error is not only in the highest degree prophylactic, but it serves as a stimulating introduction to the study of truth." *Walter Lippman*

"There is no mistake so great as that of being always right." *Samuel Butler*

The stakes of mistakes tend to grow with the ability to make difficult choices. This means that making decisions unfortunately does not tend to get easier as abilities improve. Always expect to encounter tough choices…. *K.M.T.*

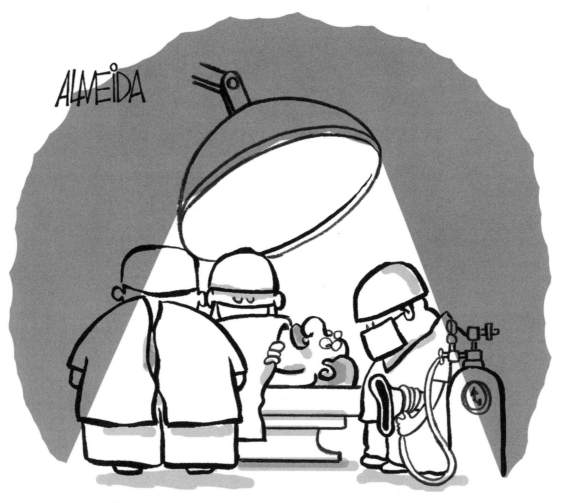

"You better start counting sheep,
this thing doesn't seem to be working!"

"CONTRARY TO ALL THESE REPORTS ON DOCTOR ERRORS, MR. JOHNSON, YOUR SURGERY WAS PERFORMED COMPETENTLY AND PUNCTUALLY, AS MY WATCH CLEARLY INDICATES."

"It would be a great honor for me to be counted as one of your successes."

"This is a second opinion. At first, I thought you had something else."

"Either this is the wrong chart or—let's just hope this is the wrong chart."

"FIND OUT WHO SET UP THIS EXPERIMENT. IT SEEMS THAT HALF OF THE PATIENTS WERE GIVEN A PLACEBO, AND THE OTHER HALF WERE GIVEN A DIFFERENT PLACEBO."

"If I knew where I'd <u>lost</u> the sponge, it wouldn't be <u>lost</u>, now, would it?"

"DON'T FORGET — KEEP THE POTASSIUM CHLORIDE IN A SEPARATE CONTAINER."

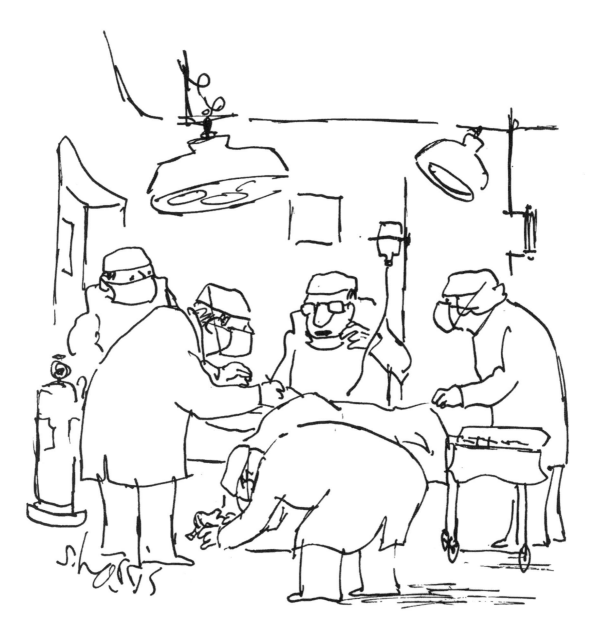

"ALL RIGHT, SO HE DROPPED THE HEART. THE FLOOR IS CLEAN."

"He's one tough cookie. I've never seen anyone bounce back from an autopsy before."

"*Next, an example of the very same procedure when done correctly.*"

-6-
Choices and Risk Trade-offs

Choices represent the options in decisions that may lead to trade-offs of risks. Some risk trade-offs transfer and/or transform the risks, and they can be tough to see. Watch out!

***

"All substances are poisonous, there is none which is not a poison; the right dose differentiates a poison from a remedy." *Paracelsus*

"Credit is not given for work not in on time." *Ida Henrietta Hyde*

"I shall be telling this with a sigh
 Somewhere ages and ages hence:
 Two roads diverged in a wood, and I -
 I took the one less traveled by,
 And that has made all the difference." *Robert Frost*

"There is a way of looking at life called 'keeping things in perspective.' This simply means 'making yourself feel better by comparing the things that are happening to you right now against other things that have happened at a different time, or to different people.' For instance, if you were upset about an ugly pimple on the end of your nose, you might try to feel better by keeping your pimple in perspective. You might compare your pimple situation to that of someone who was being eaten by a bear, and when you looked in the mirror at your ugly pimple, you could say to yourself, 'Well, at least I'm not being eaten by a bear.' You can see at once why keeping things in perspective rarely works very well, because it is hard to concentrate on somebody else being eaten by a bear when you are staring at your own ugly pimple." *Lemony Snicket*

"Obviously, a man's judgment cannot be better than the information on which he has based it." *Arthur Hays Sulzberger*

"The consequences of our actions are always so complicated, so diverse, that predicting the future is a very difficult business indeed." *J.K. Rowling*

"Interdependence. Not just one thing leading to another in a straight line, but everything and everyone everywhere interreacting." *Madeline L'Engle*

"History teaches us that men and nations behave wisely once they have exhausted all the other alternatives." *Abba Eban*

"An appeaser is one who feeds a crocodile hoping it will eat him last." *Sir Winston Churchill*

"A ship in port is safe, but that is not what ships are for. Sail out to sea and do new things." *Grace Murray Hopper*

"A man cannot be too careful in the choice of his enemies." *Oscar Wilde*

"Proverbial wisdom counsels against risk and change. But sitting ducks fare worst of all." *Mason Cooley*

"Our passional nature not only lawfully may, but must, decide an option between propositions, whenever it is a genuine option that cannot by its nature be decided on intellectual grounds; for to say, under such circumstances, 'Do not decide, but leave the question open,' is itself a passional decision - just like deciding yes or no - and is attended with the same risk of losing the truth." *William James*

"If man is not ready to risk his life, where is his dignity?" *André Malraux*

"If we want to solve a problem that we have never solved before, we must leave the door to the unknown ajar." *Richard P. Feynman*

"It is better to risk saving a guilty person than to condemn an innocent one." *Voltaire*

"Everybody knows if you are too careful you are so occupied in being careful that you are sure to stumble over something." *Gertrude Stein*

"Interested in understanding and even applying risk theory to better your life? I'll give you a moment to match the risks with the rewards." *Bob Berger*

"When you are safe at home, you wish you were having an adventure; when you're having an adventure, you wish you were safe at home." *Thorton Wilder*

"Put all your eggs in the one basket and - WATCH THAT BASKET." *Mark Twain*

"Technology ... is a queer thing. It brings you great gifts with one hand, and it stabs you in the back with the other." *C.P. Snow*

"The word 'risk' derives from the early Italian *risicare*, which means 'to dare.' In this sense, risk is a choice rather than a fate. The actions we dare to take, which depend on how free we are to make choices, are what the story of risk is all about. And that story helps define what it means to be a human being." *Peter L. Bernstein*

"Scientists know that they will sometimes be wrong; they try not to err too often, but they accept some insecurity as the price of the wider scope." *John W. Tukey*

Those who believe in the Myth of Zero Risk experience great difficulty upon encountering the Law of Unintended Consequences. *K.M.T.*

"*In your case, Dave, there's a choice—elective surgery, outpatient medicinal therapy, or whatever's in the box that our lovely Carol is holding.*"

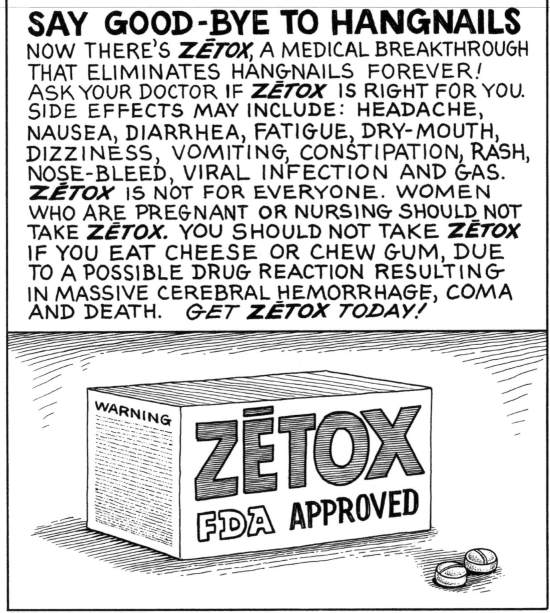

"Don't forget to take a handful of our complimentary antibiotics on your way out."

Choices and Risk Trade-offs

"Look, I'd like to avoid overkill, but not at the risk of underkill."

"THE SNICKERS AND SWEETARTS LOOK CLEAN, BUT I'M GOING TO IRRADIATE THE GUMMY BEARS JUST TO BE ON THE SAFE SIDE."

"You've been fooling around with alternative medicines, haven't you?"

"Paper or plastic?"

"Don't you think it's about time
you got a babysitter?"

"JUST ANOTHER COUPLE OF PAGES."

"Even more dangerous than crossing the road is being undercooked."

"*And then one day I decided that not taking risks was the greatest risk of all.*"

"Maybe zero tolerance is setting the bar too high."

"We've got to draw a line on unethical behavior and then get as close to that line as possible."

-7-
Effectiveness, Benefits, and Costs

Effectiveness represents a critical concept in answering the question: "How well will it work?" We assess the benefits and costs of options by quantifying the pros and cons, usually in terms of money. Thus, these concepts go one step beyond choices and risk trade-offs.

***

"Remember that time is money." *Benjamin Franklin*

"Life itself still remains a very effective therapist." *Karen Horney*

"The right word may be effective, but no word was ever as effective as a rightly timed pause." *Mark Twain*

"An effective human being is a whole that is greater than the sum of its parts." *Ida P. Rolf*

"Children's talent to endure stems from their ignorance of alternatives." *Maya Angelou*

"It is surprising what money I have spent out of a principle of economy; because they are cheap I have bought more shoes than a millipede could wear in VII years. By my caps you would think I had more heads than a Hydra." *Elizabeth Montagu*

"The discovery of truth is prevented more effectively, not by the false appearance things present and which mislead into error, not directly by weakness of the reasoning powers, but by preconceived opinion, by prejudice." *Arthur Schopenhauer*

"Economic distress will teach men, if anything can, that realities are less dangerous than fancies, that fact-finding is more effective than fault-finding." *Carl Lotus Becker*

"Strength can always be used to destroy as well as to create." *Madeline L'Engle*

"All progress is based upon a universal innate desire on the part of every organism to live beyond its income." *Samuel Butler*

"There are risks and costs to a program of action. But they are far less than the long-range risks and costs of comfortable inaction." *John F. Kennedy*

"Those who thoughtlessly make use of the miracles of science and technology, without understanding more about them than a cow eating plants understands about botany, should be ashamed of themselves." *Albert Einstein*

"No one can build his security upon the nobleness of another person." *Willa Cather*

"'This is a radiator,' Aunt Josephine said.... 'Please don't ever touch it. You may find yourself very cold here in my home. I never turn on the radiator, because I am frightened that it might explode, so it often gets chilly in the evenings.... This is the telephone.... It should only be used in emergencies, because there is a danger of electrocution.... When you open this door, just push on the wood here. Never use the doorknob. I'm always afraid that it will shatter into a million pieces and that one of them will hit my eye.... Those cans? For burglars, naturally.... You must be as afraid of burglars as I am. So every night, simply place these tin cans by the door, so that when burglars come in, they'll trip over the cans and you'll wake up.... Actually, it's not hot soup. I never cook anything hot because I'm afraid of turning the stove on. It might burst into flames. Oh, I could never sell this house, ... I'm terrified of realtors.'" *Lemony Snicket*

"If we open a quarrel between the past and the present, we shall find that we have lost the future." *Sir Winston Churchill*

"It's a funny thing, the less people have to live for, the less nerve they have to risk losing-nothing." *Zora Neale Hurston*

"To save all we must risk all." *Friedrich von Schiller*

"One cannot collect all the beautiful shells on the beach." *Anne Morrow Lindbergh*

"You see things; and you say, 'Why?' But I dream things that never were; and I say, 'Why not?'" *George Bernard Shaw*

"You will never be happy if you continue to search for what happiness consists of. You will never live if you are looking for the meaning of life." *Albert Camus*

"I'm not afraid of storms, for I'm learning how to sail my ship." *Louisa May Alcott*

"The years teach much which the days never know." *Ralph Waldo Emerson*

"When a fellow says, it hain't the money but the principle o' the thing, it's th' money." *Frank McKinney "Kin" Hubbard*

"It is easier to resist at the beginning that at the end." *Leonardo da Vinci*

"Example is always more efficacious than precept." *Samuel Johnson*

"Government is more than the sum of all the interests; it is the paramount interest, the public interest. It must be the efficient, effective agent of a responsible citizenry, not the shelter of the incompetent and the corrupt." *Adlai Stevenson*

Resources are limited, so plan accordingly. *K.M.T.*

© 12/17/97 Jim Borgman, Cincinnati Enquirer. Reprinted with special permission of King Features Syndicate.

Wellness Update: Thirty-year-old man starting on the twenty-five-thousand-pound oat-bran muffin he must consume over forty years in order to reduce significantly his risk of death from high cholesterol

LOUIS PASTEUR, AFTER DISCOVERING THAT MICROBES TRANSMITTED DISEASE, EXPERIMENTED WITH METHODS FOR KILLING THEM

"*And, in our continuing effort to minimize surgical costs, I'll be hitting you over the head and tearing you open with my bare hands.*"

SCOTT WILLIS / *Mercury News Editorial Cartoonist*

© 11/10/99 Jim Borgman, Cincinnati Enquirer. Reprinted with special permission of King Features Syndicate.

© 12/19/99 Jim Borgman, Cincinnati Enquirer. Reprinted with special permission of King Features Syndicate.

"I WANT TO BE THIN LIKE ALLY McBEAL, STACKED LIKE BARBIE and ETERNALLY YOUNG LIKE A SUPERMODEL.... NOW IF YOU'LL EXCUSE ME, I HAVE TO GO VOMIT MY HAPPY MEAL. "

Effectiveness, Benefits, and Costs   145

Effectiveness, Benefits, and Costs   147

Choices in Sex Education

"BUT IT WOULDN'T BE EASY TO GET EVERYONE TO WEAR IT ALL THE TIME."

"I'd have been here sooner if it hadn't been for early detection."

"Larry just LOVES messing with people in the risk assessment profession!"

"It's a new anti-depressant—instead of swallowing it, you throw it at anyone who appears to be having a good time."

"On the one hand, eliminating the middleman would result in lower costs, increased sales, and greater consumer satisfaction; on the other hand, we're the middleman."

"Trust me Mort—no electronic-communications superhighway, no matter how vast and sophisticated, will ever replace the art of the schmooze."

"Oh, O.K. Well, when your family's all through hunkering down, then can Timmy come out and play?"

Effectiveness, Benefits, and Costs   157

-8-
Values and Preferences

Values represent our assessment of the worth of things, both tangible and intangible, while preferences dictate our relative desires for different things when we compare and decide.

***

"When the well's dry, we know the worth of water." *Benjamin Franklin*

"[J]ust as it is the white man's way to assert himself in any landscape, to change it, make it over a little (at least to leave some mark of memorial of his sojourn), it was the Indian's way to pass through a country without disturbing anything; to pass and leave no trace, like fish through the water, or birds through the air." *Willa Cather*

"What is a cynic?… A man who knows the price of everything and the value of nothing." *Oscar Wilde*

"It matters not how a man dies, but how he lives." *Samuel Johnson*

"At every step the child should be allowed to meet the real experiences of life; the thorns should never be plucked from his roses." *Ellen Key*

"It is not in giving life but in risking life that man is raised above the animal; that is why superiority has been accorded in humanity not to the sex that brings forth but to that which kills." *Simone de Beauvoir*

"Art is long, life short; judgment difficult, opportunity transient." *Johann Wolfgang von Goethe*

"I feel no need for any other faith than my faith in human beings." *Pearl S. Buck*

"That mysterious independent variable of political calculation, Public Opinion." *Thomas Henry Huxley*

"'It is not respectable,' she said. And when people say that, it's no use anyone's saying anything." *Edith Nesbit*

"Nothing is more dangerous in wartime than to live in the temperamental atmosphere of a Gallup Poll, always feeling one's pulse and taking one's temperature." *Sir Winston Churchill*

"Courage is the price that life exacts for granting peace.
The soul that knows it not, knows no release" *Amelia Earhart Putnam*

"The chief value of money lies in the fact that one lives in a world in which it is overestimated." *H.L. Mencken*

"Parentage is a very important profession; but no test of fitness for it is ever imposed in the interest of the children." *George Bernard Shaw*

"Delay is preferable to error." *Thomas Jefferson*

"Society chooses to disregard the mistreatment of children, judging it to be altogether normal because it is so common place." *Alice Miller*

"The difference between the first and second best things in art absolutely seems to escape verbal definition - it is a matter of a hair, a shade, an inward quiver of some kind - yet what miles away in point of preciousness!" *William James*

"We do not choose survival as a value; it chooses us." *Burrhus Frederic Skinner*

"Always do right. This will gratify some people, and astonish the rest." *Mark Twain*

"It is our task in our time and in our generation to hand down undiminished to those who come after us, as was handed down to us by those who went before, the natural wealth and beauty which is ours." *John F. Kennedy*

"For the children and the flowers are my sisters and my brothers,
  their laughter and their loveliness would clear a cloudy day.
  Like the music of the mountains and the colors of the rainbow
  they're a promise of the future and the blessing for today." *John Denver*

"It is our responsibility as scientists, knowing the great progress and great value of a satisfactory philosophy of ignorance, the great progress that is the fruit of freedom of thought, to proclaim the value of this freedom, to teach how doubt is not to be feared but welcomed and discussed, and to demand this freedom as our duty to all coming generations." *Richard P. Feynman*

"Money can't buy me love." *John Lennon and Paul McCartney*

"We have to do the best we can. This is our sacred human responsibility." *Albert Einstein*

"The values by which we are to survive are not rules for just and unjust conduct, but are those deeper illuminations in whose light justice and injustice, good and evil, means and ends are seen in fearful sharpness of outline." *Jacob Bronowski*

"Come! Let us be off. It is foolish to conjure up woe where none exists." *Christopher Paolini*

"… nothing satisfied me. Each joy made me seek another." *Albert Camus*

Values are best taught by example and understood through observation. *K.M.T.*

"My opinion? Gee, that's a toughie. Can you give me a hint?"

"I'm a social scientist, Michael. That means I can't explain
electricity or anything like that, but if you ever want to know
about people I'm your man."

"Loving involves risk, but Michael and I are pretty courageous people."

"Hendricks, I just heard someone say that the best things in life AREN'T THINGS! Find out *what* they are, *who* has them, and then make an immediate cash offer for the entire lot!"

© 6/8/97 Jim Borgman, Cincinnati Enquirer. Reprinted with special permission of King Features Syndicate.

© 7/10/99 Jim Borgman, Cincinnati Enquirer. Reprinted with special permission of King Features Syndicate.

"I keep my core beliefs written on my palm for easy reference."

"It appears that you'll definitely outlive your usefulness."

"IGNORE ME."

"I HAVEN'T HAD A MINUTE TO MYSELF RECENTLY. I'M ON ONE COMMITTEE WHICH IS TRYING TO DETERMINE WHEN HUMAN LIFE BEGINS, ANOTHER COMMITTEE SEARCHING FOR THE MEANING OF LIFE, AND A THIRD COMMITTEE WHICH IS TRYING TO DETERMINE WHEN LIFE IS LEGALLY OVER."

"THE ENVIRONMENT PEOPLE ONLY WORRY ABOUT ENDANGERED SPECIES, NOT ENDANGERED INDIVIDUALS."

"I PREFER THESE IMPORTED CIGARETTES —
THEY DON'T HAVE A HEALTH WARNING."

"Please, Doc—nothing too aggressive. I'm kind of attached to my symptoms."

"I'm sorry, I didn't hear what you said. I was listening to my body."

"YOU SHOULD ALL GET ALONG BEAUTIFULLY. FRED HANDLES TOXIC WASTES, DORIS WORKS AT A NUCLEAR REACTOR AND WALTER JUST ISN'T TAKING ANY CHANCES."

"LOOK AT THE IRREGULAR COLORS, THE ODD SHAPES, THE WORM HOLES..."

"Now, of the twelve drugs we've tested on you, which one tasted best?"

"WHAT'LL IT BE — ONE LARGE RISK OR SEVERAL SMALL ONES?"

"*I have no particular <u>objection</u> to the earth, but I wouldn't go so far as to call myself its friend.*"

"LAB ANIMALS THE WORLD OVER WILL BE GRATEFUL FOR WHAT YOU'RE ABOUT TO DO."

-9-
Risks in the Media

This book strives to communicate effectively about risk. Most people get information from a wide range of sources including books, but the popular electronic media continue to represent the leading resource.

Reporters face significant challenges when talking and writing about risks and grappling with uncertain science. They want to develop a good and catchy story, break it first, and provide accurate and useful information. With today's around-the-clock news, it's a tough job. Reporters must quickly synthesize information, significantly distill it down, and repackage it for their intended audience. With real space constraints, either in air time or number of printed words, reporters must decide what makes it into the story, and this inevitably means that some context gets omitted. Every year, I require the public health students in my class to find an article in the popular press based on a scientific study, and to review both it and the original study (see page 314). This always proves an eye-opening experience, in part because without realizing it we often assume that when we hear something reported it must be true. Entertainment media also play important roles in people's lives, and too often people consume media uncritically. They fail to ask important questions about the media, and to pay careful attention to their media diet. Thus, while media represent pervasive, persuasive, and powerful teachers that strongly influence our perceptions of risk, they often do so under the radar screen. Consume media critically and pay very close attention to how media messages influence you.

***

"Who steals my purse steals trash - 'tis something, nothing;
'Twas mine, 'tis his, and has been slave to thousands;
But he that filches from me my good name
Robs me of that which not enriches him
And makes me poor indeed." *William Shakespeare*

"Those who corrupt the public mind are just as evil as those who steal from the public purse." *Adlai Stevenson*

"We have a natural right to make use of our pens as of our tongue, at our peril, risk, and hazard." *Voltaire*

"These remarks should make clear that motion pictures are a genuine educational institution; not educational in the restricted and conventional sense of supplying to the adolescent some detached bit of knowledge, …but educational in the truer sense of actually introducing him to and acquainting him with a type of life which has immediate, practical, and momentous significance." *Herbert Blumer*

"Everybody gets so much information all day long that they lose their common sense." *Gertrude Stein*

"Without criticism and reliable and intelligent reporting, the government cannot govern." *Walter Lippmann*

"You can fool too many of the people too much of the time." *James Thurber*

"In America, public opinion is the leader." *Frances Perkins*

"I keep six honest serving men
(They taught me all I knew);
Their names are What and Why and When
And How and Where and Who" *Rudyard Kipling*

"A journalist is the lookout on the bridge of the ship of state. He notes the passing sail, the little things of interest that dot the horizon in fine weather. He reports the drifting castaway whom the ship can save. He peers through fog and storm to give warning of dangers ahead. He is not thinking of his wages or the profits of his owners. He is there to watch over the safety and welfare of the people who trust him." *Joseph Pulitzer*

"Jounalism over here [in America] is not only an obsession but a drawback that cannot be overrated. Politicians are frightened of the press, and in the same way as bull-fighting has a brutalizing effect on Spain (of which she is unconscious), headlines of murder, rape, and rubbish, excite and demoralize the American public." *Margot Asquith*

"Ought we not to ask the media to agree among themselves a voluntary code of conduct, under which they would not say or show anything which could assist the terrorists' morale or their cause while the hijack lasted?" *Margaret Thatcher*

"The press, which is mostly controlled by vested interests, has an excessive influence on public opinion." *Albert Einstein*

"One of the basic troubles with radio and television news is that both instruments have grown up as an incompatible combination of show business, advertising and news. Each of the three is a rather bizarre and demanding profession. And when you get all three under one roof, the dust never settles." *Edward Murrow*

"A reporter must always guard against reporting the plausible as the actual, and this is certainly true in foreign affairs. What is likely or logical does not always happen in foreign policy; reporting likelihoods as facts before they come true is not far removed, it seems to me, from other kinds of misreporting." *Robert J. Manning*

"Once a newspaper touches a story, the facts are lost forever, even to the protagonists." *Norman Mailler*

"It is a newspaper's duty to print the news and raise hell." *Wilbur F. Storey*

"Back in the 1960s, a man named Sullivan had sued the *New York Times* over defamation of character, and had demonstrated that the newspaper had not been entirely correct in its commentary. But the paper had argued, and the court had agreed, that in the absence of true malice, the mistake was not really culpable, and that the public's interest in learning the goings-on in their nation superseded protection of an individual…. The First Amendment guaranteed freedom of the press, and the reason for it was that the press was America's first and, in many ways, only guardian of freedom. People lied all the time. Especially people in government, but others, too, and it was the job of the media to get the facts - the *truth* - out to the people, so that they could make their own choices…. The media could destroy people. There was recourse against almost any improper action in American society, but reporters had such protections as those once enjoyed by kings, and as a practical matter, [journalism] was above the law. As a practical matter, also, it worked hard to stay that way. To admit error was not only a legal faux pas, for which money might have to be paid. It would also weaken the faith of the public … so [journalists] never admitted error when they didn't have to, and when they did, the retractions were almost never given the prominence of the initial, incorrect, assertions - the minimum necessary effort defined by lawyers who knew exactly the height of the castle walls they defended." *Tom Clancy*

"Cartoon animation offers a medium of story telling and visual entertainment which can bring pleasure and information to people of all ages everywhere in the world." *Walt Disney*

"Many journalists continue to believe that they are involved in a calling so high as to entitle them to rights not given ordinary citizens, among them the right to deceive without consequence." *Dorothy Rabinowitz*

"Every journalist who is not too stupid or too full of himself to notice what is going on knows that what he does is morally indefensible. He is a kind of confidence man, preying on people's vanity, ignorance, or loneliness, gaining their trust and betraying them without remorse." *Janet Malcolm*

"Whether plucked from a press conference or a barroom conversation, quotes are not just reported - they're selected…. [E]xcept when a newspaper prints verbatim transcripts, all quotations are taken out of context. The context is the actual conversation or press conference in which the words get uttered; the printed pages of a newspaper can only rudely duplicate it…. All quotations may be created equal, but all misquotations are not." *David Okrent*

"Q: Name the industry that, when it comes to power, lack of accountability, arrogance and the making of money in the name of sacred constitutional rights, actually makes lawyers look good…. A: Media." *Steven Brill*

"The sensible expression would be 'No news is no news,' except that it is so obvious it is hardly an expression at all." *Lemony Snicket*

Education versus entertainment stands as a great false dichotomy, perhaps on the level of nature versus nurture. Learning happens. *K.M.T.*

© 5/13/97 Jim Borgman, Cincinnati Enquirer. Reprinted with special permission of King Features Syndicate.

"I CAN'T MAKE A STATEMENT TO THE PRESS. THAT WOULD VIOLATE THE CONFIDENTIAL RELATIONSHIP BETWEEN THE RESEARCHER AND HIS GUINEA PIGS."

© 9/7/97 Jim Borgman, Cincinnati Enquirer. Reprinted with special permission of King Features Syndicate.

Amazing But Unfortunately True Department
The Pentagon Hires Hollywood Writers to Imagine Other Terror Scenarios*

© 5/20/98 Jim Borgman, Cincinnati Enquirer. Reprinted with special permission of King Features Syndicate.

© 10/31/00 Jim Borgman, Cincinnati Enquirer. Reprinted with special permission of King Features Syndicate.

"HUMAN CLONING: COULD IT HAPPEN? NEXT ON...."

© 8/15/97 Jim Borgman, Cincinnati Enquirer. Reprinted with special permission of King Features Syndicate.

© 1/1/99 Jim Borgman, Cincinnati Enquirer. Reprinted with special permission of King Features Syndicate.

© 1/12/98 Jim Borgman, Cincinnati Enquirer. Reprinted with special permission of King Features Syndicate.

© 9/08/00 Jim Borgman, Cincinnati Enquirer. Reprinted with special permission of King Features Syndicate.

"*I forget the name of the product, but the jingle on TV goes something like 'Ya-dee-dum-dee-rah-te-dum-dee-rah-dee-dum.'*"

© 6/25/01 Jim Borgman, Cincinnati Enquirer. Reprinted with special permission of King Features Syndicate.

"I think the dosage needs adjusting. I'm not nearly
as happy as the people in the ads."

MIDNIGHT IN THE GARDEN OF GOOD AND EVIL

© 5/23/99 Jim Borgman, Cincinnati Enquirer. Reprinted with special permission of King Features Syndicate.

© 8/26/99 Jim Borgman, Cincinnati Enquirer. Reprinted with special permission of King Features Syndicate.

FOXTROT © 1995 Bill Amend. Reprinted with permission of UNIVERSAL PRESS SYNDICATE. All rights reserved.

CALVIN AND HOBBES © 1995 Watterson. Reprinted with permission of UNIVERSAL PRESS SYNDICATE. All rights reserved.

"CONTRARY TO THE POPULAR VIEW, OUR STUDIES SHOW THAT IT IS REAL LIFE THAT CONTRIBUTES TO VIOLENCE ON TELEVISION."

"ALL RIGHT, IT'S A DEAL. THE FOUR-LETTER WORDS ARE IN, THE DRUG LYRICS ARE OUT."

"...NO, HE CAN'T REALLY FLY.. NO, THE BAD GUYS REALLY DON'T HAVE A RAY GUN... NO, THIS CEREAL REALLY ISN'T THE BEST FOOD IN THE WHOLE WORLD... NO, IT WON'T REALLY MAKE YOU AS STRONG AS A GIANT..."

"I UNDERSTAND THEY HAD A VERY DEPRIVED CHILDHOOD. EVERYTHING WAS IN BLACK AND WHITE."

© 7/2/01 Jim Borgman, Cincinnati Enquirer. Reprinted with special permission of King Features Syndicate.

© 2003 Walt Handelsman, Tribune Media Services, Inc. Reprinted with permission.

© 11/30/97 Jim Borgman, Cincinnati Enquirer. Reprinted with special permission of King Features Syndicate.

"*Since you have already been convicted by the media, I imagine we can wrap this up pretty quickly.*"

-10-
Risks Meet Law and Policy

The differences in the way that lawyers and scientists view evidence makes for fascinating discussions, particularly with respect to risks. With scientists always uncertain to some degree and lawyers always seeking certainty, conflicts naturally arise, and unfortuantely individuals often get caught in the middle. The main problem that arises in my view comes from the introduction of inefficient bureaucracy to deal with it all. The government clearly needs to play a role in protecting individuals, but the arguments for stepping in should require some evidence to support an argument that governmental action is both required and will be effective, which of course implies plenty of opportunities for risk analysts (and lawyers).

***

De minimis non curat lex. [The law is not concerned with trifles.]

"We need to have the spirit of science in international affairs, to make the conduct of international affairs the effort to find the right solution, the just solution of international problems, not the effort by each nation to get the better of the other nations, to do harm to them when it is possible." *Linus Carl Pauling*

"That one hundred and fifty lawyers should do business together ought not to be expected." *Thomas Jefferson*

"The church and the law deal with the yesterdays of life; medicine deals with the tomorrows." *William J. Mayo*

"The law is the last resort of human wisdom acting upon human experience for the benefit of the public." *Samuel Johnson*

"Now and then an innocent man is sent to the legislature." *Frank McKinney "Kin" Hubbard*

"Power tends to corrupt, and absolute power corrupts absolutely. Great men are almost always bad men." *John Emerich Edward Dalberg*

"Women constitute half of the population of every country. To disregard women and bar them from active participation in political, social, economic and cultural life would in fact be tantamount to depriving the entire population of every society of half its capability." *Shirin Ebadi*

"Advice is what we ask for when we already know the answer but wish we didn't…." *Erica Jong*

"You must do the thing you think you cannot do." *Eleanor Roosevelt*

"Government is everywhere to a great extent controlled by powerful minorities, with an interest distinct from that of the mass of the people." *Goldsworthy Lowes Dickinson*

"Facts are stubborn things; and whatever may be our wishes, our inclinations, or the dictates of our passions, they cannot alter the state of facts and evidence." *John Adams*

"When the President does it, that means it is not illegal." *Richard Nixon*

"The less government we have, the better - the fewer laws, and the less confided power." *Ralph Waldo Emerson*

"We must not read either law or history backwards." *Helen M. Cam*

"Diplomats make it their business to conceal the facts." *Margaret Sanger*

"Every dictator uses religion as a prop to keep him in power." *Benazir Bhutto*

"As citizens of this democracy, you are the rulers and the ruled, the lawgivers and the law-abiding, the beginning and the end." *Adlai Stevenson*

"Let us never negotiate out of fear, but let us never fear to negotiate." *John F. Kennedy*

"Old forms of government finally grow so oppressive that they must be thrown off even at the risk of reigns to terror." *Herbert Spencer*

"We are becoming the servants in thought, as in action, of the machine we have created to serve us." *John Kenneth Galbraith*

"Good laws lead to the making of better ones; bad ones bring about worse." *Jean Jacques Rousseau*

"After all, that is what laws are for, to be made and unmade." *Emma Goldman*

"How amazing it is that, in the midst of controversies on every conceivable subject, one should expect unanimity of opinion upon difficult legal questions! … The history of scholarship is a record of disagreements. And when we deal with questions relating to principles of law and their applications, we do not suddenly rise into a stratosphere of icy certainty." *Charles Evans Hughes*

"Law, by definition, cannot obey the same rules as nature." *Albert Camus*

"The law hath not been dead, though it hath slept." *William Shakespeare*

"Our civilization is shifting from science and technology to rhetoric and litigation." *Mason Cooley*

The standards applied for determining the acceptability of risk and the associated tolerances for uncertainty and error depend on the forum in which the case is considered. K.M.T.

© 7/6/97 Jim Borgman, Cincinnati Enquirer. Reprinted with special permission of King Features Syndicate.

© 11/20/00 Jim Borgman, Cincinnati Enquirer. Reprinted with special permission of King Features Syndicate.

"With all these lectures and safety manuals, I'm about ready for a <u>trip</u> to where I can lie down and forget about all these rules and regulations!"

Clay Bennett 1999 © The Christian Science Monitor.

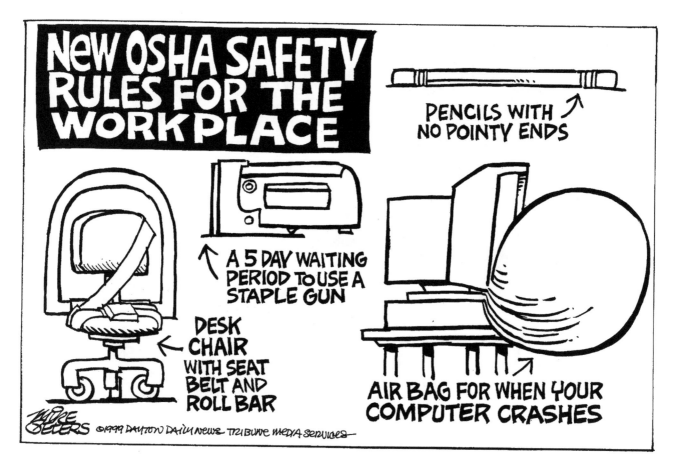

"So *that's* where it goes! Well, I'd like to thank you fellows for bringing this to my attention."

© 2003 Sidney Harris. Reprinted with permission from Sidney Harris.

"I THOUGHT HE WOULD RUN ALL SORTS OF SCIENTIFIC TESTS."

"THE FOOD AND DRUG ADMINISTRATION IS REALLY CRACKING DOWN. WE HAVE TO LIST ALL THE INGREDIENTS IN OUR POTIONS."

U.S. Park Service May Have Started Fire That Destroyed Los Alamos

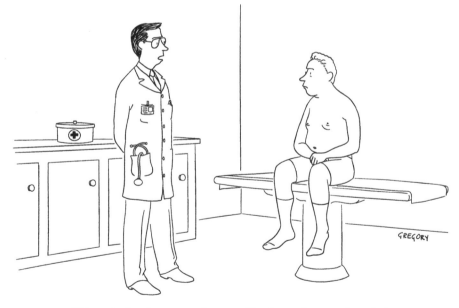

"Your infection may be antibiotic-resistant, but let's see how it responds to intensive litigation."

"We medical practitioners do our very best, Mr. Nyman. Nothing is more sacred to us than the doctor-plaintiff relationship."

"The doctor is in court on Tuesdays and Wednesdays."

"I'll want to run a few tests on you, just to cover my ass."

"It's a baby. Federal regulations prohibit our mentioning its race, age, or gender."

"*Your mother and I still think two dollars a week is plenty, but, in an effort to avoid litigation, we're willing to go to two seventy-five.*"

"*Your Honor, we're going to go with the prosecution's spin.*"

"Tarzan hate frivolous lawsuits."

"Apparently, you have very little respect for our judicial system, sauntering in here with only one lawyer."

"Look, I'm not blaming you. I'm just suing you."

"Someday, all of this liability exposure will be yours!"

-11-
Health Care in the U.S.

The U.S. system of health care remains one of the most complicated and perplexing in the world. Without universal care, the U.S. continues to provide care for some and not for others, but the rules of the game evolve as rapidly as the science that drives health care. In the past year, the U.S. government grappled with the issue of paying for pharmaceuticals for seniors and issues related to Americans importing cheaper drugs from other countries. We lead the world in innovation when it comes to new pharmaceutical products as researchers discover new "magic pills," while at the same time some basic public health interventions remain underutilized.

The paradox of the best system for some, but inadequate care for others, combined with ever-increasing costs and complexity creates many humorous perspectives. With respect to your own health, you must recognize that you are responsible for yourself and act accordingly. Your decisions matter, so don't forget to ASK QUESTIONS! When it comes to public health, you must recognize that decisions made by others also matter for you.

***

"The first possibility of rural cleanliness lies in *water supply.*" *Florence Nightingale*

"Life is the risk we cannot refuse." *Mason Cooley*

"Disease creates poverty and poverty disease. The vicious circle is closed." *Henry E. Sigerist*

"Thus everything is on the side of the doctor. When men die of disease they are said to die from natural causes. When they recover (and they mostly do) the doctor gets the credit of curing them." *George Bernard Shaw*

"Better to hunt in the fields, for health unbought,
  Than fee the doctor for a nauseous draught.
  The wise, for cure, on exercise depend;
  God never made his work for men to mend." *John Dryden*

"He's the best physician that knows the worthlessness of the most medicines." *Benjamin Franklin*

"The essential principles of health are not understood by the people… and alas! not by all our physicians, who as a rule have been educated to cure disease, not to prevent it. Too many have been taught to fight Nature's Laws, not to stand by… as her adjutant." *Ellen Swallow*

"A physician who treats himself has a fool for a patient." *William Osler*

"The aim of medicine is to prevent disease and prolong life; the ideal of medicine is to eliminate the need of a physician." *William J. Mayo*

"Medicine is the science of uncertainty and an art of probability." *Emily Mumford*

"There is no cure for birth and death save to enjoy the interval." *George Santayana*

"If you believe the doctors, nothing is wholesome; if you believe the theologians, nothing is innocent; if you believe the soldiers, nothing is safe." *Robert Arthur Talbot Gascoyne-Cecil*

"Who shall decide when doctors disagree?" *Alexander Pope*

"A physician's business is to avert disease, to heal the sick, to prolong life, and to diminish suffering." *Oliver Wendell Holmes*

"We recommend that no one eat more than two tons of turkey - that's what it would take to poison someone." *Elizabeth Whelan*

"Whenever there is a contingency, the cheapest way of providing against it is by uniting with others, so that each man may subject himself to a small deprivation, in order that no man may be subjected to a great loss. He, upon whom the contingency does not fall, does not get his money back again, nor does he get from it any visible or tangible benefit, but he obtains security against ruin and consequent peace of mind. He, upon whom the contingency does fall, gets all that those whom fortune has exempted from it have lost in hard money, and is thus enabled to sustain an event which would otherwise overwhelm him." *Select Committee of the House of Commons*

"It is incident to physicians, I am afraid, beyond all other men, to mistake subsequence for consequence." *Samuel Johnson*

"But my words have been un-heeded. It was still too early, and because of this they still could not meet with full understanding. It shared the fate of so many similar cases in medicine, where a long time has also been necessary before old prejudices were overcome and the new facts were acknowledged to be correct by the physicians." *Robert Koch*

"I suppose one has a greater sense of intellectual degradation after an interview with a doctor than from any human experience." *Alice James*

"The best doctors in the world are Doctor Diet, Doctor Quiet, and Doctor Merryman." *Jonathan Swift*

"The worth is in the act. Your worth halts when you surrender the will to change and experience life. But options are before you; choose one and dedicate yourself to it. The deeds will give you new hope and purpose." *Christopher Paolini*

It's time to put the public back into public health. *K.M.T.*

ELDON FLAGLER WAS AWARDED the NOBEL PRIZE FOR MEDICINE TODAY FOR DISCOVERING HOW TO GET HIS HMO TO PAY FOR an OVERNIGHT HOSPITAL STAY FOLLOWING QUADRUPLE BYPASS SURGERY.

**"What do you mean, I have an ulcer?
I give ulcers, I don't get them!"**

*"Doctors said that although the approach is still experimental, it may prove
an effective weapon in the fight against health-care reform."*

"O.K., you be the doctor, and I'll be the Secretary of Health and Human Services."

246   Risk in Perspective

"Ah, Mr. Bromley. Nice to put a face on a disease."

**"These tests are completely unnecessary.
I just want to see how your insurance reacts."**

"I SEE YOUR INSURANCE COVERS LITTLE GREEN PILLS, LITTLE YELLOW PILLS, LITTLE WHITE PILLS, LITTLE RED PILLS AND LITTLE PURPLE PILLS. WHAT I'M GOING TO GIVE YOU ARE SOME LITTLE ORANGE PILLS."

MANY YEARS LATER

"*My third felony was a smart move. Folks on the outside are still waiting for health care.*"

"*I'm sorry. The doctor no longer makes phone calls.*"

"Next, I will use a medium-point roller-ball pen with black ink and, on the anterior side of the upper-left quadrant, two centimetres below the binding staple, begin detailing in bold print the patient's previous medications and treatments relating to present indications for procedure and treatment, as required on this particular health-insurance form."

"*This patient has a rare form of medical insurance.*"

**"On your way out perhaps you'd like Nurse Miller
to show you our complete line of health foods
and tell you about our new health club center."**

*"I have no objection to alternative medicine so long as traditional
medical fees are scrupulously maintained."*

"*Our integrated approach to medicine skillfully combines an array of holistic alternative treatments with a sophisticated computerized billing service.*"

"*I'm sorry, the doctor no longer makes diagnoses.*"

"Under our holistic approach, Mr. Wyndot, we not only treat your symptoms, we also treat your dog."

"Well, as we thought, it's something gross."

"You're not ill yet, Mr. Blendell, but you've got potential."

"To relieve the pressure of your medical bills, I'm going to recommend that we go ahead and drain your savings account."

"Mr. Wilkins, I believe that your condition is going to get us both into the 'Journal of the American Medical Association.' "

"According to an article in the upcoming issue of 'The New England Journal of Medicine,' all your fears are well founded."

"My doctor says you should be drawing more fruits and vegetables."

-12-
Signs of the Times

Rapid evolution leads to many interesting glimpses of the world at any point in time. Enjoy!

***

"He was a bold man that first ate an oyster." *Jonathan Swift*

"To give an accurate description of what has never occurred is not merely the proper occupation of the historian, but the inalienable privilege of any man of parts and culture." *Oscar Wilde*

"Of all cooperative enterprises, public health is the most important and gives the greatest returns." *William J. Mayo*

"I don't know everything. I just do everything." *Toni Morrison*

"Can anybody remember when the times were not hard and money not scarce?" *Ralph Waldo Emerson*

"I know what it means to be a miner and a cowboy, and have risked my life when need be, *but*, best of all, I have felt the charm of the glorious freedom, the quick rushing blood, the bounding motion of the wild life, the joy of the living and of the doing, of the mountain and the plain; I have learned to know and feel some, at least, of the secrets of the Wild Ones." *Grace Seton-Thompson*

"Unless the vast forests of the United States can be made ready to meet the vast demands which this [economic] growth will inevitably bring, commercial disaster, that means disaster to the whole country, is inevitable. The railroads must have ties.... If the present rate of forest destruction is allowed to continue, with nothing to offset it, a timber famine in the future is inevitable." *Theodore Roosevelt*

"Ages of faith and disbelief are always said to mark the course of history." *Edith Hamilton*

"The fruits of the tree of knowledge are various; he must be strong indeed who can digest all of them...." *Mary Coleridge*

"Knowledge and timber shouldn't be much used until they are seasoned." *Oliver Wendell Holmes*

"Be not afraid of life. Believe that life is worth living, and your belief will help create that fact." *William James*

"If a little knowledge is dangerous, where is there the man who has so much as to be out of danger?" *Thomas Henry Huxley*

"I think something is only dangerous if you are not prepared for it or if you don't have control over it or if you can't think through how to get yourself out of a problem." *Judith Resnik*

"In the progress of politics, as in the common occurrences of life, we are not only apt to forget the ground we have traveled over, but frequently neglect to gather up experiences as we go." *Thomas Paine*

"It is strange that science, which in the old days seemed harmless, should have evolved into a nightmare that causes everyone to tremble." *Albert Einstein*

"We saw the risk we took in doing good,
  But dared not spare to do the best we could
  Though harm should come of it" *Robert Frost*

"...I was taught that the way of progress is neither swift nor easy." *Marie Curie*

"All art requires courage." *Anne Tucker*

"Move With the Cheese And Enjoy It!" *Stephen Johnson*

Top Ten Signs that we live in the Age of Risk Management:
10. The president declares that ridge measurement is the key to homestyle deference (meaning that risk management is the key to homeland defense).
9. California voters realize that every single object in a hardware store poses a potential risk of injury and place Proposition 10,000,065 on the ballot to require labeling on every individual item, thus threatening the ability of Californians to purchase nails in quantities of less than 1,000,000.
8. Public support of Proposition 10,000,065 appears to wane as California homeowners find themselves more concerned with informing each other that every home contains mold and that even organic food contains trace levels of naturally occurring elements like lead, cadmium, mercury, and arsenic as a result of growing on Earth. Search for an alternative planet continues.
7. Toothpicks come in paper or plastic.
6. The size of toothpick packages must be increased to contain a statement that the "Surgeon General warns that toothpicks can cause severe injury when used improperly." Product managers fear loss of brand recognition and reporters begin investigating injuries for an exposé.
5. Patients go to their doctors with non-specific symptoms and concern that they might have caught one of the most feared viruses now circulating - an Internet virus.
4. Bill Gates foresees the first transmission of an Internet virus from a computer to a person and begins a drive for a vaccine to protect children in the developing world from this horrible fate - finally accepting that his corporate and philanthropic efforts will inevitably align completely.
3. Feature movies appear with risk analysts as main characters.
2. Risk Analysts Without Borders opens its doors.
1. The David Letterman show comes up with its own funnier, shorter, and way better list. *K.M.T.*

*"Years ago, there was only one Santa Claus. Now because
of genetic engineering, there can be lots of them."*

"And it was so typically brilliant of you to have invited an epidemiologist."

"Sir, the following paradigm shifts occurred while you were out."

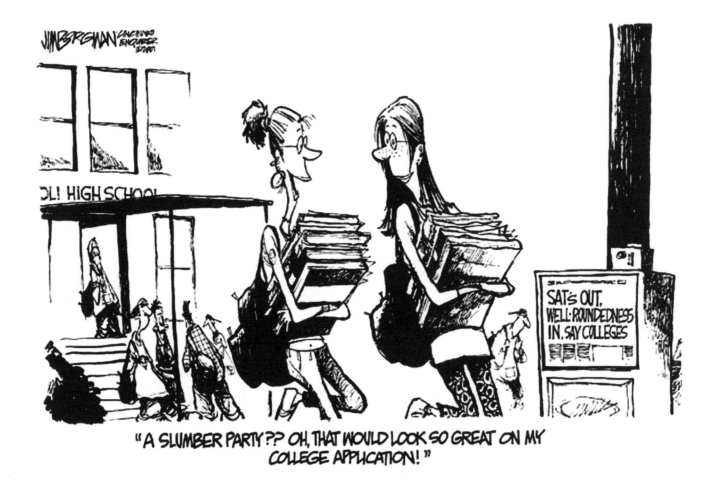

© 3/19/01 Jim Borgman, Cincinnati Enquirer. Reprinted with special permission of King Features Syndicate.

"...AND THIS IS WHERE MY DAD KEEPS THE GUN THAT WE DON'T KNOW ABOUT."

"*You have the right to remain silent. Anything you say may be used against you in a court of law, newspapers, periodicals, radio, television, all electronic media, and technologies yet to be invented.*"

© 6/4/99 Jim Borgman, Cincinnati Enquirer. Reprinted with special permission of King Features Syndicate.

© 2003 Sidney Harris. Reprinted with permission from Sidney Harris. All rights reserved.

© 10/29/99 Jim Borgman, Cincinnati Enquirer. Reprinted with special permission of King Features Syndicate.

"OK, I'LL MOVE BALLET BACK AN HOUR, RESCHEDULE GYMNASTICS, and CANCEL PIANO...YOU SHIFT YOUR VIOLIN LESSON TO THURSDAY and SKIP SOCCER PRACTICE...... THAT GIVES US FROM 3:15 TO 3:45 ON WEDNESDAY THE 16TH TO PLAY."

"It's very important that you try very, very hard to remember where you electronically transferred Mommy and Daddy's assets."

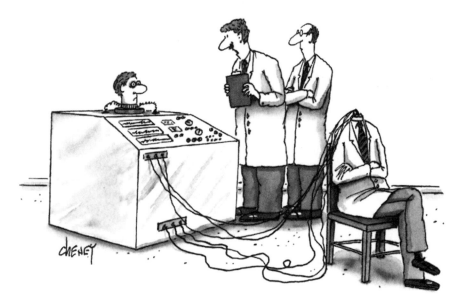

"Bad news, Phil—due to federal funding cutbacks, we can't afford to put your head back on."

© 5/27/98 Jim Borgman, Cincinnati Enquirer. Reprinted with special permission of King Features Syndicate.

"Don't be downhearted, Larry. I believe that when life slams a door in your face, it always opens another one for you somewhere else!"

"Hey, I've operated on this guy before—there are my initials."

"*Certainly. A party of four at seven-thirty in the name of Dr. Jennings. May I ask whether that is an actual medical degree or merely a Ph.D.?*"

"She's the most effective of our emerging new pathogens."

"NOW I'M HAVING TROUBLE DOING HYPOTHETICAL EXPERIMENTS ON PRIMATES."

"If it's a choice between ethical behavior and increased profits, we must ask what's best for the shareholders."

"And a final note: today, at 3:28 P.M. Beltway time, perception officially became reality."

© 1/19/00 Jim Borgman, Cincinnati Enquirer. Reprinted with special permission of King Features Syndicate.

"WOULD YOU LIKE THAT TO BE A STEAK WITH A BROAD-SPECTRUM ANTIBIOTIC, OR ONE WITH A VARIETY OF THERAPEUTIC PROTEINS?"

"THE LOWER-PRICED ITEMS CONTAIN GENETICALLY-MODIFIED FOODS NOT YET APPROVED FOR HUMAN USE."

"IF YOU'D LIKE TO, YOU CAN DISCUSS THE QUESTION OF EATING GENETICALLY-MODIFIED FOOD WITH OUR STAFF ETHICIST."

"Do you, Cynthia, who is completely free of any genetic engineering, take Rodney, who is equally free . . ."

"SO— ANYONE ELSE WANT TO BE GENETICALLY MODIFIED?"

"WE JUST DON'T GET INVOLVED WITH THINGS LIKE DOUBLE-BLIND TESTS AND PEER REVIEW. WE'RE JUST A LITTLE MOM-AND-POP LABORATORY."

"WHAT'S BECOME OF ALL THE VISIBLE RISKS: SPEEDING TRUCKS, FIRES, FLOODS? NOW IT'S ALL GENES, RADIATION AND CHEMICAL SUBSTANCES."

"THE RISK-BENEFIT ANALYSIS SAYS NO, THE COST-BENEFIT ANALYSIS SAYS MAYBE, AND MY GUT FEELING SAYS 'GO FOR IT'!"

Epilogue

"After all, tomorrow is another day." *Margaret Mitchell*

"What is not recorded is not remembered." *Benazir Bhutto*

"Colin Powell's Rules:
1. It ain't as bad as you think. It will look better in the morning.
2. Get mad, then get over it.
3. Avoid having your ego so close to your position that when your position falls, your ego goes with it.
4. It can be done!
5. Be careful what you choose. You may get it.
6. Don't let adverse facts stand in the way of a good decision.
7. You can't make someone else's choices. You shouldn't let someone else make yours.
8. Check small things.
9. Share credit.
10. Remain calm. Be kind." *Colin Powell*

"Life is what happens to you while you're busy making other plans." *John Lennon*

"When we remember we are all mad, the mysteries disappear and life stands explained." *Mark Twain*

"Things are always at their best in their beginning." *Blaise Pascal*

"Now is not the end. It is not even the beginning of the end. But it is, perhaps, the end of the beginning." *Sir Winston Churchill*

"The wave of the future is coming and there is no fighting it." *Anne Morrow Lindbergh*

"There are two kinds of fears: rational and irrational - or, in simpler terms, fears that make sense and fears that don't." *Lemony Snicket*

"Work hard. Tell everyone everything you know. Close a deal with a handshake. Have fun." *Harold "Doc" Edgerton*

"May the force be with you." *George Lucas*

"That's all there is, there isn't any more." *Ethel Barrymore*

Thank you. *K.M.T.*

"HERE YOUR ETERNITY WILL BE FREE FROM ANY AND ALL BOTHERSOME UNCERTAINTY ABOUT DEATH, AND WE GUARANTEE YOU WILL REST WITH A PEACE LIKE YOU'VE NEVER KNOWN, OR YOUR MONEY BACK. YOU CAN CHOOSE BETWEEN CERTAINTY LANE, INFINITY ORCHARD OR OUR DECISION-FREE HAVEN..."

Index of Quotes

Feynman, Richard P., *The Pleasure of Finding Things Out*, 1999
Fleming, Sir Alexander, Address at Edinburgh University, 1951
Galilei ,Galileo, Letter to the Grand Duchess Christina of Tuscany, 1615
Goethe, Johann Wolfgang von, Letter to Karl Friedrich Zelter, 1812
Hamilton, Alice, *Exploring the Dangerous Trades*, 1943
Hamilton, Edith, *The Roman Way*, 1932
Huxley, Thomas Henry, *Our Knowledge of the Causes of the Phenomena of Organic Nature*, 1863
Kepler, Johannes, *Somnium*, 1634
L'Engle, Madeline, *Introduction to A Wrinkle in Time*, 1997
Lessing, Doris, *The Four-Gated City*, 1969
Mead, Margaret, *Coming of Age in Samoa*, 1928
Newton, Sir Isaac, *Brewster, Memoirs of Newton*, 1855
Pauling, Linus Carl, *No More War!* 1958
Planck, Max, *The Philosophy of Physics*, 1936
Ride, Sally, *To Space and Back*, 1986
Roddenbury, Gene, opening for *Star Trek*, 1966
Sagan, Carl, *Cosmos*, 1980
Snow, C.P. (Charles Percy), "The Two Cultures," *The New Statesman and Nation*, 1956
Teller, Edward, *The Pursuit of Simplicity*, 1981
Whitehead, A.N. (Alfred North), *Science and the Modern World*, 1925
Wilde, Oscar, *The Importance of Being Earnest*, 1895

Chapter 2

Butler, Samuel, *Samuel Butler's Notebooks*, 1912
de Laplace, Pierre, *Ouevres*, 1812-1820
Eddington, Sir Arthur Stanley, *The Scientific Monthly*, 1950
Edison, Thomas, *Life*, 1932
Farmer, Fannie, *The Boston Cooking-School Cookbook*, 1896
Feynman, Richard P., *The Pleasure of Finding Things Out*, 1999
Friedman, Milton and L.J. Savage, *Journal of Political Economy*, 1948
Fuller, Richard Buckminster, *The Prospect for Humanity*, 1964
Galilei, Galileo, *Il Saggiatore*, 1623
Hawking, Stephen W., *A Brief History of Time: From the Big Bang to Black Holes*, 1988
Johnson, Samuel, Letter to Boswell, 1787
Keynes, John Maynard, *A Tract on Monetary Reform*, 1923
Maxwell, James Clerk, *On Faraday's Lines of Force*, 1856
Morawetz, Cathleen Synge, American Mathematical Society Retiring Presidential Address, 1997
Nightingale, Florence, Letter to Dr. William Farr, 1874
Pascal, Blaise, *Pensées*, 1670
Peters, John Punnett, *Yale Journal of Biology and Medicine*, 1953
Raiffa, Howard, *Decision Analysis: Introductory Lectures on Choices under Uncertainty*, 1968
Russell, Bertrand, *The Study of Mathematics*, 1902
Schwartz, Lisa et al., *Annals of Internal Medicine*, 1997
Thomson, William [Lord Kelvin], *Popular Lectures and Addresses*, 1891-94
Tukey, John W., *Annals of Mathematical Statistics*, 1962
Tversky, Amos and Daniel Kahneman, *Psychological Bulletin*, 1971
von Neumann, John, 1951, Quoted in *The Art of Computer Programming, Vol. II*, 1968

Chapter 3

Barr, Amelia E., *All the Days of My Life*, 1913

Bartlett, Elisha, *An Essay on the Philosophy of Medical Science*, 1844

Churchill, Sir Winston, *Step By Step 1936-1939*, 1939

Colette, *My Mother's House*, 1922

Darwin, Charles, *The Origin of Species*, 1859

Dick, Philip K., *The Minority Report*, 1991

Hamilton, Edith, *The Greek Way*, 1930

Hungerford, Margaret Wolfe, *Molly Brown*, 1878

Johnson, Samuel, *The Idler*, 1758-60

Leslie, Amy, *Amy Leslie at the Fair*, 1893

Montagu, Elizabeth, Letter to Mrs. Robinson, 1810-13

Morrison, Toni, *The New York Times*, 1986

National Research Council, *Science and Judgment in Risk Assessment*, 1994

O'Connor, Sandra Day, *Phoenix Magazine*, 1971

Osler, William, *Boston Medical and Surgical Journal*, 1903

Parton, Dolly, *Coat of Many Colors*, 1994

Peter, Laurence J., *The Peter Principle*, 1969

Porter, Sylvia, *Sylvia Porter's Money Book*, 1975

Somerville, Mary, *Physical Geography*, 1848

Tarbell, Ida M., *All in the Day's Work*, 1939

Tucker, Sophie, *Some of These Days*, 1945

Twain, Mark, Answering a toast "To the babies," 1879

Chapter 4

Bergamín, José, *El Cohete y La Estrella*, 1923

Butler, Samuel, Notebooks, *Life*, 1912

Churchill, Sir Winston, Radio Broadcast, 1939

Darwin, Charles, *Life and Letters of Charles Darwin*, 1887

da Vinci, Leonardo, *Treatise on Painting*, 1651

Dillard, Annie, *Pilgrim at Tinker Creek*, 1974

Doyle, Sir Arthur Conan, *The Sign of the Four*, 1890

Einstein, Albert, in "Geometry and Experience" speech in Berlin, 1921

Feynman, Richard P., *The Pleasure of Finding Things Out*, 1999

Frost, Robert, *The Road Not Taken*, 1916

Holmes, Oliver Wendell, Jr., *The Path of the Law*, 1897

James, William, *The Will to Believe*, 1897

Jefferson, Thomas, *Notes on the State of Virginia*, 1781-85

Johnson, Samuel, *The Idler*, 1758-60

Keller, Helen, *The Open Door*, 1957

Montgomery, Lucy, *Anne of Green Gables*, 1908

Moroney, M.J., *Facts from Figures*, 1951

Persegati, Walter, *The New York Times*, 1984

Richards, Peter, *Learning Medicine*, 1985

Tukey, John W., *Annals of Mathematical Statistics*, 1962

Twain, Mark, *Life on the Mississippi*, 1883

Weed, Lawrence L., Lecture to the New York Academy of Family Physicians, 1996

von Goethe, Johann Wolfgang, *Maxims and Reflections*, 1829
Wilson, Woodrow, *Mere Literature and Other Essays*, 1896

Chapter 5
Amiel, Henri-Frédéric, *Journal Intime*, 1852
Bohr, Niels, in Mackay, A., *The Harvest of a Quiet Eye*, 1977
Butler, Samuel, *Samuel Butler's Notebooks*, 1951
Commoner, Barry, *The Closing Circle: Nature, Man, and Technology*, 1971
Doyle, Sir Arthur Conan, *On the Interpretation of Nature*, 1753
Feynman, Richard P., *The Pleasure of Finding Things Out*, 1999
Hugo, Victor, *Les Misérables*, 1862
Huxley, Thomas Henry, *The Coming of Age of the Origin of Species*, 1880
Jefferson, Thomas, *Notes on the State of Virginia*, 1787
Lippmann, Walter, *Public Opinion*, 1922
McClintock, Barbara, *Time*, 1983
Nash, Ogden, *Marriage Lines: Notes of a Student Husband*, 1964
Paine, Thomas, *Common Sense*, 1776
Pascal, Blaise, *Pensées*, 1670
Pope, Alexander, *An Essay on Criticism*, 1711
Santayana, George, *The Life of Reason*, 1905-6
Sayers, Dorothy L., *In the Teeth of the Evidence, and Other Stories*, 1939
Shakespeare, William, *Julius Caesar*, 1598-1600
Shaw, George Bernard, *The Doctor's Dilemma*, 1913
Thompson, Sir D'Arcy Wentworth, *On Growth and Form*, 1917
von Goethe, Johann Wolfgang, *Faust*, 1808-32
Wilde, Oscar, *Lady Windermere's Fan*, 1892

Chapter 6
Berger, Bob, *Beating Murphy's Law: The Amazing Science of Risk*, 1994
Bernstein, Peter L., *Against the Gods: The Remarkable Story of Risk*, 1996
Churchill, Sir Winston, in *Reader's Digest*, 1954
Cooley, Mason, *City Aphorisms*, 1986
Eban, Abba, in a Speech in London, 1970
Feynman, Richard Philips, *The Pleasure of Finding Things Out*, 1999
Frost, Robert, *The Road Not Taken*, 1916
Hopper, Grace Murray, in *A Kick in the Seat of the Pants*, 1986
Hyde, Ida Henrietta, *Outlines of Experimental Physiology*, 1905
James, William, *The Will to Believe*, 1897
L'Engle, Madeline, *A Swiftly Tilting Planet*, 1978
Malraux, André, *Man's Fate (La Condition Humaine)*, 1936
Paracelsus, *Seven Defensiones*, circa 1538
Rowling, J.K., *Harry Potter and the Prisoner of Azkaban*, 1999
Snicket, Lemony, *The Wide Window*, 2000
Snow, C.P. (Charles Percy), *The New York Times*, 1971
Stein, Gertrude, *Everybody's Autobiography*, 1937
Sulzberger, Arthur Hays, in a speech to New York State Publishers Association, 1948

Huxley, Thomas Henry, *Universities, Actual and Ideal*, 1874
James, William, in a Letter to Henry Rutgers Marshall, 1899
Jefferson, Thomas, in a Letter to George Washington, 1792
Johnson, Samuel, *Boswell's Life*, 1769
Kennedy, John F., in Speech at the National Wildlife Federation Building, 1961
Key, Ellen, *The Century of the Child*, 1909
Lennon, John and Paul McCartney, "Can't Buy Me Love," 1964
Mencken, H.L. (Henry Lewis), *The Vintage Mencken*, 1956
Miller, Alice, *Pictures of Childhood*, 1986
Nesbit, Edith, *The Five Children and It*, 1902
Paolini, Christopher, *Eragon*, 2003
Shaw, George Bernard, *Everybody's Political What's What*, 1944
Skinner, Burrhus Frederic, in a Television Program, 1971
Twain, Mark, in a Card sent to the Young People's Society, 1901
von Goethe, Johann Wolfgang, *Wilhelm Meisters Lehrjahre*, 1786-1830
Wilde, Oscar, *Lady Windermere's Fan*, 1893

Chapter 9
Asquith, Margot, *My Impressions of America*, 1922
Blumer, Herbert, *Movies and Conduct*, 1933
Brill, Steven, Letter from Steven Brill posted on *Brill's Content* website, 1998
Clancy, Tom, *Executive Orders*, 1996
Disney, Walt, *The Quotable Walt Disney*, 2001
Einstein, Albert, *Ideas and Opinions*, 1936
Kipling, Rudyard, *The Just-So Stories*, 1902
Lippmann, Walter, in a speech to the International Press Institute Assembly, 1965
Mailler, Norman, *Esquire*, 1960
Malcolm, Janet, *The Journalist and the Murderer*, 1990
Manning, Robert J., in *The Responsibility of the Press*, 1966
Murrow, Edward, in *The Responsibility of the Press*, 1966
Okrent, David, *The New York Times*, 2004
Perkins, Frances, *People at Work*, 1934
Pulitzer, Joseph, *The North American Review*, 1904
Rabinowitz, Dorothy, *The Wall Street Journal*, 1997
Shakespeare, William, *Othello*, 1604-5
Snicket, Lemony, *The Hostile Hospital*, 2001
Stein, Gertrude, *Reflection on the Atomic Bomb*, 1973
Stevenson, Adlai, in a speech in Albuquerque, NM, 1952
Storey, Wilbur, Statement of the Aims of the Chicago Times, 1861
Thatcher, Margaret, in a speech in London, 1985
Thurber, James, *Fables for Our Time*, 1940
Voltaire, *Dictionnaire Philosophique*, 1764

Chapter 10
Adams, John, in Defense of the Soldiers in the Boston Massacre Trials, 1770
Bhutto, Benazir, *Daughter of Destiny*, 1989
Cam, Helen M., *Introduction to Selected Essays of F.W. Martland*, 1936

Camus, Albert, *Resistance, Rebellion and Death*, 1961

Cooley, Mason, *City Aphorisms*, 1987

Dalberg, John Emerich Edward, 1887, in *The Life and Letters of Mandell Creighton*, 1904

Dickinson, Goldsworthy Lowes, *The Choice Before Us*, 1917

Ebadi, Shirin, from her Nobel Peace Prize Lecture, 2003

Emerson, Ralph Waldo, *Essays, Second Series*, 1844

Galbraith, John Kenneth, *The New Industrial State*, 1967

Goldman, Emma, in *The Social Aspects of Birth Control in Mother Earth*, 1916

Hubbard, Frank McKinney "Kin", *Abe Martin's Broadcast*, 1930

Hughes, Charles Evans, in a Speech to American Law Institute, 1936

Jefferson, Thomas, *Autobiography*, 1821

Johnson, Samuel, Mrs. Piozzi, *Anecdotes of Samuel Johnson*, 1786

Jong, Erica, *How to Save Your Own Life*, 1977

Kennedy, John F., Inaugural Address, 1961

Mayo, William J., *Collected Papers May Clinic and Mayo Foundation*, 1931

Nixon, Richard, 1977, quoted in *I Gave Them A Sword*, 1978

Pauling, Linus Carl, *No More War!*, 1958

Roosevelt, Eleanor, *You Learn By Living*, 1960

Rousseau, Jean Jacques, *Du Contrat Social*, 1762

Sanger, Margaret, *Women and the New Race*, 1920

Spencer, Herbert, *Essays on Education*, 1861

Stevenson, Adlai, in a speech in Chicago, IL, 1952

Shakespeare, William, *Measure for Measure*, 1604-5

Chapter 11

Cooley, Mason, *City Aphorisms*, 1994

Dryden, John, *Epistle to John Driden of Chesterton*, 1700

Franklin, Benjamin, *Poor Richard's Almanac*, 1733

Gascoyne-Cecil, Robert Arthur Talbot, Marquess of Salisbury, in Letter to Lord Lytton, 1877

Holmes, Oliver Wendell, *Medical Essays, Scholastic and Bedside Teaching*, 1891

James, Alice, 1890, *The Diary of Alice James*, 1964

Johnson, Samuel, in *Literary Magazine*, 1756

Koch, Robert, in his Nobel Lecture, 1905

Mayo, William J., *Proceedings of the National Education Association*, 1928

Mumford, Emily, *Interns: From Students to Physicians*, 1970

Nightingale, Florence, in a Letter to Medical Officer of Health, 1891

Osler, William, edited by Bean, William, *Aphorisms*, 1950

Paolini, Christopher, *Eragon*, 2003

Pope, Alexander, *Moral Essays*, 1732

Santayana, George, *Soliloquies in England and Later Soliloquies*, 1922

Select Committee of the House of Commons, 1825

Shaw, George Bernard, *The Doctor's Dilemma*, 1913

Sigerist, Henry E., *Medicine and Human Welfare*, 1941

Swallow, Ellen, *The New England Kitchen Magazine*, 1893

Swift, Jonathan, *Polite Conversation*, 1738

Whelan, Elizabeth, *US News & World Report*, 1986

Chapter 12

Coleridge, Mary, *Gathered Leaves from the Prose of Mary Coleridge*, 1910
Curie, Marie, *Pierre Curie*, 1923
Einstein, Albert, to Queen Elizabeth of Belgium, 1954
Emerson, Ralph Waldo, *Society and Solitude*, 1870
Frost, Robert, *Mountain Interval*, 1916
Hamilton, Edith, *Witness to the Truth*, 1948
Holmes, Oliver Wendell, *The Autocrat of the Breakfast Table*, 1858
Huxley, Thomas Henry, *On Elemental Instruction in Physiology*, 1877
James, William, *The Will to Believe*, 1897
Johnson, Stephen, *Who Moved My Cheese?* 1998
Mayo, William J., in *Collected Papers of the Mayo Clinic and Mayo Foundation*, 1919
Morrison, Toni, *Sula*, 1974
Paine, Thomas, *Common Sense*, 1777
Resnik, Judith, *Time*, 1986
Roosevelt, Theodore in a speech to the American Forest Congress, 1905
Seton-Thompson, Grace, *A Woman Tenderfoot*, 1900
Swift, Jonathan, *Polite Conversation*, 1738
Tucker, Anne, *The Woman's Eye*, 1973
Wilde, Oscar, *Intentions*, 1891

Epilogue

Barrymore, Ethel, added at the end of Sunday, 1906
Bhutto, Benazir, *Daughter of Destiny*, 1989
Churchill, Sir Winston, in a speech at the Lord Mayor's Day Luncheon, 1942
Edgerton, Harold "Doc," Motto displayed in Strobe Alley at MIT
Lennon, John, *"Beautiful Boy (Darling Boy),"* 1980
Lindbergh, Anne Morrow, *The Wave of the Future*, 1940
Lucas, George, *Star Wars*, 1977
Mitchell, Margaret, *Gone with the Wind*, 1936
Pascal, Blaise, *Lettres Provinciales*, 1656-7
Powell, Colin, *My American Journey*, 1995
Snicket, Lemony, *The Wide Window*, 2000
Twain, Mark, *Notebook*, 1898

Index of Cartoons by Artist

Extras

1. Improving Public Understanding: Guidelines for Communicating Uncertain Science on Nutrition, Food Safety, and Health (Reprinted with permission from the International Food Information Council), pages 308-313

2. Exercises, pages 314-322

3. Debunked and uncertain quotes, pages 323-324

4. About the author, page 325

COMMENTARY

Improving Public Understanding: Guidelines for Communicating Emerging Science on Nutrition, Food Safety, and Health

For Journalists, Scientists, and All Other Communicators

Based on an advisory group convened by the Harvard School of Public Health and the International Food Information Council Foundation*

Twenty-five years ago, the chances were slim that a food and health-related study in a scientific journal would make the evening news or greet readers in their morning newspapers. Now, hardly a week goes by when a breaking dietary study doesn't make headlines.

There are a number of reasons why. Public interest in nutrition and food safety has increased dramatically. And food stories—because they are inherently so personal—make for compelling news. Just as important, scientists have much to gain from increased visibility. And the same holds true for the journals that first publish the studies or other communicators who have an interest in advancing public understanding of the issues.

But there's another reality about emerging science, the media, and the public. And that's confusion. Surveys tell us that the high volume of media coverage has not brought clarity to or improved understanding of a topic of such obvious impact. More has not always meant better.

Again, there are several reasons why. First, the public's unfamiliarity with the scientific process can make the evolutionary nature of research appear contradictory and confusing. Second, scientists, themselves, don't always agree on what constitutes scientific evidence sufficient to warrant changing recommendations to the public. And, perhaps most important of all, how emerging science is communicated—by scientists, the journals, the media, and the many interest groups that influence the process—also can have powerful effects on the public's understanding, on its behavior and, ultimately, on its well-being.

To examine these issues and assist the communications process, the Harvard School of Public Health and the International Food Information Council Foundation convened an advisory group of leading experts. Following the initial meeting in Boston, Massachusetts, a series of eight roundtables was held around the country involving more than 60 other nutrition researchers, food scientists, journal editors, university press officers, broadcast and print reporters, consumer groups, and food industry executives. (See "Appendix" section.)

Based on input from the participants at these meetings, a set of guiding principles for the communication of emerging science has been developed. The first draft of guidelines was subsequently reviewed by a second meeting of advisory group members and revised, and the final draft circulated to roundtable participants prior to publication. At the heart of these principles is the belief that food-related science *can* be effectively communicated in ways that serve both public understanding and the objectives of the communicators.

Of all the questions surrounding the communication of food-related studies, perhaps the most basic is, should single studies be communicated at all to the public at large? Almost by definition, much of the information involved is preliminary, not conclusive, and therefore not a strong basis for change in public policy or behavior. Even so, these studies, and the news stories they spawn, can be useful in raising public awareness of key nutrition, health, and food safety issues—*if* they are expressed in enough context to enable the average person to weigh the information appropriately.

These guidelines are intended to suggest how that context can be provided. They outline the necessary data, disclosures, and contextual qualifiers to help the public evaluate a study's relevance and importance. However, there is no expectation that every news story will include all or most of the suggested information. Instead, these guidelines can help communicators focus on the most vital information the public should have in order to form the most useful net impression of a particular study's findings.

With each study, the information will vary. The key to evaluating one study may be the limitations of its methodology; for another, it may be an understanding of which population groups are most affected by the findings. These guidelines will help communicators ask key questions so that they can identify which specific answers will best inform the public.

**Correspondence to:* Amelia Morgan, International Food Information Council Foundation, 1100 Connecticut Ave., N.W., Suite 430, Washington, DC 20036.

Publisher's note: Individuals and organizations are authorized and encouraged to reproduce and distribute this document, in whole or in part, without cost or permission, provided the following conditions are met: 1) The *Journal of the National Cancer Institute* is cited as the original source and 2) any parts of the document used are reproduced without alteration to the text.

The guidelines are presented in several groupings—first, general guidelines relevant for all, followed by more specific guidelines for scientists, journal editors, journalists, and interest groups. They purposely are expressed as questions, rather than imperative statements, to encourage self-inquiry and suggest measures of responsible communication. As such, they are intended to help ensure that sound science and improved public understanding are the ultimate guides to what is communicated and how.

HARVEY V. FINEBERG
SYLVIA ROWE

Advisory Group

Marcia Angell, M.D.
The New England Journal of Medicine

Elaine Auld, M.P.H.
Society for Public Health Education

David Baron
National Public Radio

Julianne Chappell
Journal of the National Cancer Institute

Harvey V. Fineberg, M.D., Ph.D., M.P.H.
Harvard School of Public Health

Beverly Freeman
Harvard School of Public Health

Jeanne Goldberg, Ph.D., R.D.
Tufts University
School of Nutrition Science and Policy

Mary Ann Howkins
Glamour

Timothy Johnson, M.D., M.P.H.
ABC News

George Lundberg, M.D.
Journal of the American Medical Association

Amelia Morgan
International Food Information Council Foundation

Michael Mudd
Kraft Foods

Richard Nelson
Monsanto

Tom Paulson
Seattle Post-Intelligencer

David Rosenthal, M.D.
American Cancer Society/Harvard University Health Services

Sylvia Rowe
International Food Information Council Foundation

Walter Willett, M.D., Dr.P.H.
Harvard School of Public Health

Margaret Winker, M.D.
Journal of the American Medical Association

Mary Winston, Ed.D.
American Heart Association

General Guidelines for ALL PARTIES in the Communications Process

1. Will your communication enhance public understanding of diet and health?
   - Is the study credible enough to warrant public attention?
   - With the information you provided, will the public be able to properly assess the importance of the findings and whether they should have any immediate bearing on their food choices?
   - Have you avoided an overly simplistic approach that may inappropriately characterize individual foods, ingredients, or supplements as good or bad? Have you helped the public understand how the food, ingredient, or supplement can be consumed as part of a total healthful diet, or why it should not be consumed?
   - Have you appropriately represented the study's overall conclusions and avoided highlighting selective findings which, on their own, might present a misleading picture?

2. Have you put the study findings into context?
   - If the findings are preliminary and nonconclusive, have you made that clear?
   - If the findings differ with previous studies, have you indicated this and explained why? If the results refute previously released results, do you provide a weight of evidence comparable to the earlier findings?
   - Have you clarified to whom the findings apply? Have you avoided generalizing the effects when the study was restricted to populations of a certain age or sex or with specific genetic, environmental, or other predisposing conditions?
   - Have you included information about risk/benefit trade-offs of consuming or not consuming certain foods, ingredients, or supplements? Have you explained how these risks and benefits compare with other factors (e.g., level of physical activity, genetic history) that may also contribute to health?
   - In explaining a dietary risk, have you distinguished between population-wide estimates and individual risk? Have you cited statistics on absolute risk and not just relative risk, e.g., expressing an increase in incidence from "one in a million to three in a million" and not just as "three times the risk"?

3. Have the study or findings been peer-reviewed?
   - Has the study been peer-reviewed by independent scientists or published in a peer-reviewed journal? At the same time, have you understood that while peer review is an important standard, it does not guarantee the findings are definitive or conclusive?
   - If a study has not been peer-reviewed (e.g., a paper presented at a meeting or convention), are the findings so important that they should be communicated to the public before peer review?
   - Have you distinguished between actual study findings and editorials or commentaries that may have been written about the study? Have you clarified that an editorial is an expression of personal views and has not always been peer-reviewed? Have you investigated how widely held these views are or whether the editorial represents a narrowly-held opinion?

4. Have you disclosed the important facts about the study?
   - Have you provided adequate information on the study's original purpose, research design, and methods of data collection and analysis?
   - Have you acknowledged any limitations or shortcomings the study may have?
5. Have you disclosed all key information about the study's funding?
   - Have you publicly disclosed all funding sources for the study?
   - Are you reasonably confident of the study's objectivity and independence?
   - Have you considered what the funders stand to gain or lose from the study's outcome?
   - Have you allowed the validity of the science to speak for itself, regardless of the funding?

Communication Guidelines for Scientists

1. Have you provided essential background information about the study in your written findings, or to journalists or others requesting it, in a language that can be understood?
   - Have you explained all details of the study including purpose, hypothesis, type and number of subjects, research design, methods of data collection and analysis, and the primary findings?
   - Are you reporting study findings consistent with the original purpose of the data collection?
   - Were appropriate scientific methods of inquiry used? Did you disclose any study shortcomings or limitations, including methods of data collection? Were objective health measurements used to help verify self-reports?
   - Was the study conducted in animals or humans? Are limitations of animal models noted in terms of their applicability to humans?
   - Have you waited to report the results until the study has been independently peer-reviewed? If not, did you disclose to the media that the findings are preliminary and have not yet been peer-reviewed?
2. Have you clarified dietary risks and benefits?
   - Did you explain the dosage of a substance or amount of food or ingredient that was linked to the health outcome? Is this amount reasonably consumed by the average individual?
   - What was the original risk of developing the disease? Have you expressed the new level of risk in terms of both absolute and relative risk?
3. Have you met the needs of the media?
   - Are you available for media interviews the day before/after the release? Do you make every attempt to respond to media inquiries in a timely fashion?
   - Does the news release prepared for the study communicate the primary findings faithfully and without exaggeration? Have you reviewed and approved the final version of your institution's news release?

Communication Guidelines for Journal Editors

1. Does your embargo policy enhance public communication?
   - Do you make embargoed copies of the journal available to all journalists who agree to respect the embargo, not just a select group of reporters?
   - Do you notify scientists whose studies will likely receive press attention when the embargoed issue is being made available?
   - Do you provide the relevant articles from the embargoed journal to study authors so they can preview other related work in that issue, helping them respond to questions?
2. Do you encourage responsible media reporting on study findings?
   - If you issue a news release on an article in your journal, is it faithful to the underlying research? Does it provide adequate background information?
3. Have you considered the effect of the study findings on consumers?
   - Have you considered what might be the effect of the study finding on the general public?
   - Does the study warrant an accompanying editorial to help put the findings into context? If so, is the editorial content included in the news release?
4. Does your submission policy permit scientists to clarify results of abstract presentations with the media?
   - Does your submission policy make it clear that scientists presenting abstracts should submit the complete report for peer review? Have you stressed they should not distribute copies of the complete report of the study, or figures or tables from that study, to the media before publication in a peer-reviewed journal?

Communication Guidelines for Journalists

1. Is your story accurate and balanced?
   - Have you established the credibility of your primary source?
   - Have you asked other reputable scientists and other third-party health sources if they believe the study is reliable and significant? Have these scientists reviewed the study?
   - Do the third-party sources you are quoting represent mainstream scientific thinking on the issue involved? If not, have you made it clear that such opinions or commentary differ from most scientific perspectives on this topic? If such opposing viewpoints are expressed by only one or two individuals, does the amount of coverage given reflect that these are clearly minority opinions?
   - Have you received and reviewed a copy of the study publication—not simply reviewed abstracts, news releases, wire reports, or other secondary sources of information?
   - After reviewing the study results and limitations, have you concluded it still warrants coverage? Have you objectively considered the possibility of not covering the study?
   - Are words used to describe the findings appropriate for the type of investigation? Cause and effect can only be shown directly in studies in which the intervention is the only variable modified between the experimental and control group.
   - Is the tone of the news report appropriate? Do you avoid using words that overstate the findings, e.g., "may" does not mean "will" and "some" people does not mean "all" or "most" people?

- Are the headlines, photo images, and graphics consistent with the findings and content of your article?
2. Have you applied a healthy skepticism in your reporting?
   - In talking to sources and reading news releases, have you separated fact versus emotion or commentary?
   - Do the study findings seem plausible?
   - Have you used any hyped or "loaded" terms in the headline or body of a report to attract public attention, e.g., "scientific breakthrough" or "medical miracle"? Does the report indirectly suggest that a pill, treatment, or other approach is a "silver bullet"?
   - Have you applied the same critical standards to all sources of information—from scientists, to public relations/press offices, to journals, to industry, to consumer and special interest groups? What does the information source have to gain if its point of view is presented? Have you considered a range of conflict-of-interest possibilities beyond dollars?
3. Does your story provide practical consumer advice?
   - Have you translated the findings into everyday consumer advice? For example, if a study reports on the effects of a specific nutrient, have you considered identifying the foods in which it is most commonly found?
   - How do action steps relate to the larger context of existing dietary guidance (e.g., Dietary Guidelines for Americans, USDA Food Guide Pyramid, importance of balance, variety, and moderation)?
   - Have you provided credible national, state, or local resources where consumers can obtain more information or assistance on the diet and health topic—especially if the findings present an immediate threat to public health and safety (such as foodborne or waterborne illness outbreak), e.g., brochures, toll-free hotlines, online resources?
4. Is your reporting grounded in basic understanding of scientific principles?
   - Are you aware of the difference between evidence and opinion? If not, have you consulted knowledgeable sources?
   - Are you familiar with the scientific method of inquiry and various terms such as hypothesis testing, control groups, randomization, double-blind study, etc.? Do you understand and communicate that science is evolutionary, not revolutionary in nature?
   - Are you familiar with different types of studies, why they are used, and the limitations of each?
   - Do you stay current on diet and health recommendations, so as to help identify the true significance of new findings?

Guidelines for Industry, Consumer, and Other Interest Groups

1. Have you provided accurate information and feedback to the media?
   - Is your news release on the study in keeping with the findings, i.e., neither exaggerates or oversimplifies nor disregards or sensationalizes the findings? Does it provide new insight or help enhance public understanding of the study results?
   - Do you tactfully correct misinformation in the media? Do you provide scientific explanations of why the story is incorrect, not simply express opinions or judgments of a few individuals? Do you follow-up with journalists to acknowledge an accurate, insightful story?
2. Do you adhere to ethical standards in providing diet and health information?
   - Do you respect the embargo placed on a study, rather than attempting to scoop or "be first with" the news?
   - Have you avoided promoting or writing news releases on studies that have not been peer-reviewed? Have you acknowledged that results that have not been scientifically reviewed are preliminary findings and do not call for a change in behavior?
   - Have you identified your organization's viewpoint and sources of funding?

List of Further Resources to Accompany the "Guidelines for Communicating Emerging Science on Nutrition, Food Safety, and Health"

Books

- Blum D, Knudson M, editors. A field guide for science writers. New York: Oxford University Press, 1997.
- Cohn V. News & numbers: a guide to reporting statistical claims and controversies in health and other fields. Revised ed. Ames (IA): Iowa State University Press, 1994.
- Gastel B. Presenting science to the public. Philadelphia: ISI Press, 1983.
- Kamrin MA, Katz DJ, Walter ML. Reporting on risk: a journalist's handbook on environmental-risk assessment. Los Angeles: Foundation for American Communications, 1995.
- National Association of Science Writers. Communicating science news: a guide for public information officers, scientists, and physicians. 3rd ed. Greenlawn (NY): National Association of Science Writers, 1996.
- Rodgers JE, Adams WC. Media guide for academics. Los Angeles: Foundation for American Communications, 1994.
- Shortland M, Gregory J. Communicating science: a handbook. New York: John Wiley & Sons, 1991.
- Zinsser W. On writing well: an informal guide to writing nonfiction. 5th ed. New York: Harper Perennial, 1994.
- Evered D, O'Connor M, editors. Communicating science to the public. New York: John Wiley & Sons, 1987.
- Friedman SM, Dunwoody S, Rogers CL, editors. Scientists and journalists: reporting science as news. New York: The Free Press, 1986.
- Lewenstein BV, editor. When science meets the public. Washington (DC): American Association for the Advancement of Science, 1992.
- McRae MW, editor. The literature of science: perspectives on popular scientific writing. Athens (GA): University of Georgia Press, 1993.
- Moore M, editor. Health risks and the press: perspectives on media coverage of risk assessment and health. Washington (DC): The Media Institute, 1989.
- Nelkin D. Selling science: how the press covers science and technology. Revised ed. New York: W. H. Freeman, 1995.
- Burkett W. News reporting: science, medicine, and high technology. Ames (IA): Iowa State University Press, 1986.

- Fischer HD, editor. Medicine, media and morality: Pulitzer prize-winning writings on health-related topics. Malabar (FL): Krieger Publishing Co., 1992.
- Gannon R, editor. Best science writing: readings and insights. Phoenix (AZ): Oryx Press, 1991.
- Vander AJ, Sherman JH, Luciano DS. Human physiology: the mechanisms of body function. New York: McGraw-Hill, 1985.
- Berkow R, editor. Merck manual of diagnosis and therapy. Rahway (NJ): Merck Research Laboratories, 1992.
- Larson DE, editor-in-chief. Mayo Clinic family health book. New York: William Morrow, 1990.
- Herbert V, editor. The Mount Sinai School of Medicine complete book of nutrition. New York: St. Martin's Press, October 1990.
- IFIC review: how to understand and interpret food and health-related scientific studies. International Food Information Council Foundation, July 1997.
- Dunwoody S, Crane E, Brown B. Directory of science communication courses and programs in the United States. 3rd ed. Madison (WI): Center for Environmental and Educational Studies, 1996.

Articles

- Shuchman M, Wilkes MS. Medical scientists and health news reporting: a case of miscommunication. Ann Intern Med 1997; 126:976–82.
- Multiauthored series. Medicine and the media. Lancet 1996; 347:1087–90, 1163–6, 1240–3, 1308–11, 1382–6, 1459–63, 1533–5, 1600–3.
- Taubes G. Epidemiology faces its limits. Science July 14; 1997.
- Barnes-Svarney P. Science writing today and tomorrow. The Writer 1994 Nov; 107: 15–7.
- Blakeslee A. Late night thoughts about science writing. Quill 1994 Nov/Dec;82:35–8.
- Dahir MS. Writing science & medical nonfiction: it's easier than you think. Writer's Digest 1995 Nov;75:29–31.
- Rowan KE. Strategies for explaining complex science news. Journalism Educator 1990 Summer;45:25–31.
- Miller JA. Journalist reading journals. CBE Views 1990 Apr;13:44–5.
- Ruppel-Shell E. The risks of risk studies. The Atlantic Monthly Nov;1987.
- Ross PE. Lies, damned lies & medical statistics. Forbes Aug 14;1995.

Newsletters

- ScienceWriters. Newsletter of the National Association of Science Writers.
- Sciphers. Newsletter of Science Communication Interest Group, Association for Education in Journalism and Mass Communication.
- SEJournal. Newsletter of the Society of Environmental Journalists.
- Food Insight. Newsletter of the International Food Information Council Foundation.

Workshops

- American Medical Association's Annual Medical Communications and Health Reporting Conference

Online Resources

- EurekAlert! (http://www.eurekalert.org)
- FACSNET (http://www.facsnet.org)
- National Association of Science Writers (http://www.nasw.org/)
- New England Science Writers (http://www.umass.edu/pubaffs/nesw/)
- Society of Environmental Journalists (http://www.sej.org)
- Harvard School of Public Health (http://www.hsph.harvard.edu)
- International Food Information Council Foundation (http://ificinfo.health.org)
- Tufts University Nutrition Navigator (http://navigator.tufts.edu)

Appendix

Regional Roundtable Participants

Merle Alexander
Food Writer, *The Oregonian*

David Allison, Ph.D.
Associate Research Scientist, Columbia University College of Physicians

Elaine Auld, M.P.H., C.H.E.S.
Executive Director, Society for Public Health Education, Inc.

Cathy Barber
Food Editor, *Dallas Morning News*

Cookson Beecher
Agricultural Reporter, *Capital Press*

Amy Beim
Reporter, *American Health*

Dennis Bier, M.D.
Professor of Pediatrics and Director, Children's Nutrition Research Center

Carol Brock
Food Editor, *Newark Times Ledger*

Catherine Broihier, M.S., R.D.
Freelance Writer

Nancy Byal
Executive Food Editor, *Better Homes & Gardens*

Julianne Chappell
Executive Editor, *Journal of the National Cancer Institute*

Linda Ciampa
Medical/Health Producer, *CNN-TV*

Andrea Clark
Editorial Assistant, *New Woman*

Kristine Clark, Ph.D., R.D.
Director of Sports Nutrition, Center for Sports Medicine, The Pennsylvania State University

Patricia Cobe
Freelance Writer

Anne Edelson
Public Affairs, New York University Medical Center

Karen Elam, Ph.D.
Senior Director, Consumer and Scientific Affairs, Nabisco, Inc.

Merle Ellis
Chronicle Features, San Francisco

Robert Gravani, Ph.D.
Professor of Food Science, Cornell University

Michael Greenwell
Associate Director of Health Communications, Centers for
    Disease Control and Prevention

Kate Greer
Editor, *Weight Watchers Magazine*

Phil Gunby
Director, Medical News and Humanities, *Journal of the
    American Medical Association*

Bob Hahn
Director of Legal Affairs and Research, Public Voice

Melanie Haiken
Medical/Health Editor, *Parenting*

Joanne Lamb Hayes
Food Editor, *Country Living*

Anthony Head
Diet Watch Columnist, *Bon Appetit*

James Hill, Ph.D.
Professor of Pediatrics and Medicine, University of Colorado
    Health Sciences Center

Sara Horton
Editorial Coordinator, *Arthritis Today*

Mary Ann Howkins
Food Editor, *Glamour*

Elizabeth Howze, Sc.D.
Associate Director of Health Promotion, Division of Nutrition
    and Physical Activity, Centers for Disease Control and
    Prevention

Gerard Ingenthron
Public Affairs Director, Monsanto Company

Candace Jacobs, D.V.M., M.P.H.
Assistant Director, Food Safety and Animal Health, Washington
    State Department of Agriculture

Janis Jibrin, R.D.
Freelance Nutrition Writer

Peggy Katalinich
Food Editor, *Family Circle*

Kathy Knuth
Director, Corporate Affairs, Kraft Foods

Sharon Lane
Food Editor, *Seattle Times*

Valerie Latona
Associate Editor, *Healthy Kids*

Susan Levy, M.S., R.D.
Clinical Nutritionist, New York University Medical Center

Larry Lindner
Executive Editor, *Tufts University Diet and Nutrition Letter*

Dawn Margolis
Associate Editor, *Baby Talk*

Brian McDonough, M.D.
Medical/Health Reporter, *WTXF-TV,* Channel 29 (Philadephia),
    and Chair of the National Association of Physician
    Broadcasters

Jill Melton, R.D.
Senior Food Editor, *Cooking Light*

Rochelle Melton
Assistant Editor, *Seasons Magazine*

Elaine R. Monsen, Ph.D., R.D.
Editor, *Journal of the American Diabetic Association*

Amelia Morgan
Director of Media Relations, International Food
    Information Council

Michael Mudd
Vice President, Corporate Affairs, Kraft Foods

Tom Paulson
Medical/Health Editor, *Seattle Post-Intelligencer*

Colleen Pierre, R.D.
Nutrition Writer, *Baltimore Sun*

Steve Pratt
Food Writer, *Chicago Tribune*

Frances Price, R.D.
Freelance Writer

Lawrence Proulx
Health Reporter, *Washington Post*

Elizabeth Richter
Public Television Counsultant

Sylvia Rowe
President, International Food Information Council (IFIC) and
    IFIC Foundation

Anastasia Shepers, R.D.
Assistant Editor, *Environmental Nutrition Newsletter*

Elizabeth Somer, R.D.
Author and Freelance Writer

Susan Starnes
Medical/Health Reporter, *KHOU-TV* (CBS) (Houston)

Karen Straus
Food Editor, *Vegetarian Times*

Blair Thompson
Communications Manager, Washington Dairy Products
    Commission

Connie Welch
Freelance Writer

Mary Winston, Ed.D.
Senior Science Consultant, American Heart Association

Leslie Yap
Health and Nutrition Editor, *Modern Maturity*

Exercise 1: Meeting the Press

Do you realize how many health-related headlines and sound bites bombard you? Take a look at just a few of the *USA Today* headlines that appeared in the first three months of 1999:

Town Choked by Asbestos Struggles to Overcome a Homemade Disaster
Most Families Are Doing OK, Where They Live Plays a Big Role
Pity the Poor Patient, Buried in Piles of Health-Care Paperwork
U.S. Takes Shy Step Toward Curbing Antibiotic Use on Farms
How Do We Decide Who Gets Another Chance at Life?
100,000 Infected by Blood Transfusions Go Unnoticed
Future Good Health Will Come to Those Who Listen
Questions About Thyroid Disease Still Unresolved
Study: High Fiber Diets Don't Cut Colon Cancer
Persistent Heartburn Is a Cancer Warning Sign
Education Tops List of Public's Concern in Poll
Children Not Getting Lead Tests, Study Says
Culture May Be a Key to Higher Cancer Risk
Home Radon Risk Not So High, Study Hints
No Link Found Between Fat, Breast Cancer
Despite Warnings, Toxic Shock Still a Killer
Circumcision No Longer Recommended
Weighing the Risk of a Diabetes Cure
Two Drinks a Day Keep Stroke Away
"Scars" May Be Cancer Predictor
The Side Airbag Controversy

The following activities may help you appreciate the powerful role of media in your life:

1. Search through the health-related headlines in your newspaper or your favorite news magazine. Keep a running list for a month and count the total. Also, for a few articles of interest, make a note of the headline, then read the article and see if the article matches the headline. Does it surprise you to learn that different people write the articles and headlines?

2. Read the guidelines on pages 308-313 if you skipped them. Find an interesting risk-related article from a newspaper or magazine that reports the results of a scientific study (preferably one that a peer-reviewed journal published). Get a copy of the study and the article and evaluate how well the journalist did in presenting the information compared to the criteria in the guidelines.

3. Try writing a news article limited to 200 words on a topic of interest to you. Now cut it to 100 words and evaluate what information gets lost.

4. When you see something reported inaccurately, call the reporter or write a letter to the editor.

Exercise 2: Repackaging Information

Psychological research shows that the way people perceive information depends on how it is presented. All presentations include some bias. Since most people pay more attention to things that they relate to, reporters look for a hook or anecdote to peak your interest instead of focusing on impersonal numbers and statistics. Consider the following statements and decide which would be more likely to make you want to learn more:

Baby in the neighborhood dies in sleep, or
80 out of 100,000 live births die from Sudden Infant Death Syndrome

Shooting in store kills three, or
Black males 15-19 more likely to die from guns than accidents

Tests show medication reduces symptoms by 15%, or
Local woman cured by new treatment

Sources personalize information to make it more interesting, but not everyone relates to the same things. If the story evokes a lot of emotion, think about how this affects your objectivity. If you find a story hard to read objectively, then try making it more or less personal by imagining it happening to someone else.

Your perception can also depend on whether the information is presented as positive (half-full) or negative (half-empty). Flipping the statements and looking for alternative ways to state them might change your perception. For example, if you hear about a small number of people affected, then remember that this means a large number are not affected, and vice versa.

The following activities may help you improve your repackaging information skills:

1. Try flipping these statements:
    Of all motor vehicle accidents, 90% do not involve a death.
    For most patients, a trip to the emergency room leads to full recovery.
    One out of ten people who get the disease will die from it.
    Approximately 70% of Americans wear safety belts.
    Properly used seat belts save lives.

2. Look for statements you can flip in the news or whenever you obtain information. Get into the habit of flipping them automatically.

3. When you see an anecdote used to draw your attention to a story, ask questions about the chances of the same situation happening for you. Think about the context of situations and note when you need additional information.

Exercise 3: Assessing Reliability

When evaluating reliability of information, you need to read between the lines and look for the assumptions that may make the observations more or less uncertain. For example, did the researchers assume that rats would behave the same way that humans behave? Would you have to assume that the same effects occur in women as occur in men, or occur in children as occur in adults? The main effect of assumptions comes from the uncertainty that they introduce about how well the conclusions from a sample or small set of observations apply to the larger population, even if the report sounds very certain.

Rate the following for reliability on a scale from 0 (completely unreliable) to 10 (completely reliable):
1. An anonymous e-mail message that claims an ingredient in your shampoo causes cancer.
2. A peer-reviewed paper published in a prestigious journal.
3. A report on the news about several cases of asthma that occurred in a nearby town.
4. A televised interview with a researcher who performed a study that did not show any effect of a new drug on reducing the risk of stroke.
5. A pamphlet from your doctor about ways to increase your fertility.
6. A warning label from a company about inappropriate uses of its products.
7. An advertisement that promises if you use the product you will look 10 years younger.

Think about how you can add uncertainty to discussions when you talk about things that you hear. For example, adding the preface, "I got a completely unreliable e-mail from a very reliable friend that said..." or "I read a pamphlet in my doctor's office that left me wondering about...."

Think about how you could make the following messages less or more confident?
1. This study shows that home radon risk is not high enough to warrant public concern.
2. It appears that high fiber diets reduce colon cancer risk.
3. Airbags in cars save lives.
4. Children watching too much TV might contribute to obesity.

Think about the evidence for the following health issues. Rate them on a scale from 0 (complete confidence that a health hazard does not exist) to 10 (complete confidence that a hazard does exist).
1. Dust and particles in city air and asthma
2. Global warming from carbon dioxide pollution
3. Breast implants and breast cancer
4. Radiation from medical X-rays and lung cancer
5. Natural radon in homes and buildings and lung cancer
6. Depletion of the stratospheric ozone layer and skin cancer

Consider how your uncertainty about the science might impact your receptivity to information about these. Are you skeptical or do you tend to believe everything you hear? How do you decide what and whom to believe?

Exercise 4: Getting the Numbers

Many people experience difficulty with very big and very small numbers. Consider that:

There are...

1,000,000 microseconds per second

1,000 milliseconds per second

60 seconds per minute

3600 seconds per hour

86,400 seconds per day

604,800 seconds per week

31,536,000 seconds per year

2,365,200,000 seconds expected per 75-yr life

So 1 second is...

1,000,000 or 1×10^6 microseconds

1,000 or 1×10^3 milliseconds

1/60 or 0.017 of a minute

1/3600 or 2.8×10^{-4} of an hour

1/86,400 or 1.2×10^{-5} of a day

1/604,800 or 1.7×10^{-6} of week

1/31,536,000 or 3.2×10^{-8} of a year

1/2,365,200,000 or 4×10^{-10} of a life

There are approximately ...

6,000,000,000 people in the world

290,000,000 U.S. residents

5,000,000 people in a metropolitan area

100,000 people in a suburb of a large city

10,000 people in a small city

1,000 people per small village

100 people on a short street

10 people per extended family

3 people per immediate family

2 people per couple

1 person per individual

So the chance of randomly picking 1 person is...

1/6,000,000,000 or 1.7×10^{-10}

1/290,000,000 or 3.4×10^{-9}

1/5,000,000 or 2×10^{-7}

1/100,000 or 1×10^{-5}

1/10,000 or 1×10^{-4}

1/1,000 or 1×10^{-3}

1/100 or 1×10^{-2} or 0.01 or 1%

1/10 or 0.1 or 10%

1/3 or 0.33

1/2 or 0.5

1 (People cannot be divided into smaller units)

When you receive information about large or small numbers, look for ways to put the numbers into a context that means something to you.

Estimate the numbers associated with the following questions:

1. What is the chance that someone would pick your photo out of a hat full of photos of all the members of your immediate family? How about your extended family?

2. What if they were picking your photo out of a collection of photos that included everyone who lives in your town?

3. What about picking your photo out of all the photos of people in the United States or in the world?

Exercise 5: Understanding Types of Risk

You will see all types of risk estimates reported. Some provide information about individual risks, and some focus on risks for a population. Some risk estimates provide information about short time periods, like a single event or a day, while others will focus on risks over a year or a lifetime. Finally, risk estimates might come in the form of absolute risks or relative risks. Consider these definitions that might help you sort out the different types of risks:

• **Individual risk** estimates give the chances of an outcome occurring for a particular individual or type of individual, while **population risk** estimates give the overall number of outcomes in the entire population. One way to compare a familiar individual number and a population number is to consider the difference between the amount of money that you make in a year (your individual earnings) compared to the amount of money that all Americans make in a year (the population earnings). Dividing the population earnings by the number of Americans gives the average individual earnings, and this average might be very different than your individual earnings. The average individual risk (the population risk divided by the number of members of the population) for a specific outcome might differ from your personal individual risk.

• For any risk estimate, the time period represents an important factor. You can imagine that the risk of an outcome for a single **event** or for a day might be very small, but if you experience the event frequently over time then the risk might be bigger compared to other risks. Also, during some parts of your life your risks from certain things may be higher than they are at other times. **Lifetime risk** refers to the chance that an outcome will occur at any point during your entire life.

•**Absolute risk** reflects the chance of an outcome occurring overall, while **relative risk** depends on a comparison to other numbers. Consider the difference between absolute and relative information about your earnings. For example, your absolute individual earnings might be $40,000 per year, but your relative earnings might be 1.6 times the average. Relative numbers alone might lead you to respond differently than if you also had absolute numbers. You can not possibly put relative numbers into context without absolute numbers.

Practice figuring out the type of risk information presented:
1. Consider a disease that affects only women and for which the chances of dying depend on the woman's age. Women under 40 have a 1 in 100,000 chance of dying from the disease during a year, women 40 - 65 have a 1 in 10,000 chance, and women over 65 have a 4 in 100,000 chance.
2. In the U.S. with approximately 80 million women under 40, 40 million women 40-65, and 20 million women over 65, overall approximately 5,600 women out of the 140 million women are expected to die each year. Dividing 5,600 by 140 million gives approximately 4 in 100,000.
3. Assuming that men have a risk of 0, then 5,600 Americans will die each year from the disease out of 265 million Americans. That is approximately 2 in 100,000. The annual risk for women 40 - 65 years is 10 times higher than the annual risk for women under 40.
4. Given these numbers, following a group of 140 million women from birth over the course of their lives leads to an estimate that approximately 200,000 of the 140,000,000 women (this is approximately 1 in 1,000) would die from the disease over the course of their lives. (Note that you must account for the some women die from other causes).

Exercise 6: Assessing Your Health

Think about the following potential risks and what information might help you manage them:
1. Your doctor calls to inform you that your recent blood test showed relatively high levels of cholesterol and suggests that you consider changing your diet.
2. A friend mentioned an investment that might be very lucrative if the FDA approves a new drug from a start-up company and asks you if you want to invest too.
3. A new vitamin supplement is marketed as something that will boost your energy level. You think you might benefit from it and consider buying it.

Try to be specific about the quality of your health:
Rate the quality of your health from 0 (the absolute worst) to 10 (the absolute best). Now, using the same scale, rate your health if you also experienced the following conditions.
1. A scar on your face or other minor physical disfigurement or deformity
2. A medical condition that causes mild but constant pain
3. Loss of your ability to see or hear or speak

On a scale from 0 (completely unsafe) to 10 (completely safe) rate the following activities.
1. Driving a car on the highway
2. Riding a bicycle
3. Taking a vitamin recommended by a friend
4. Smoking
5. Getting intimate with a new boyfriend or girlfriend
6. Eating fatty food

For each of these, think about two ways that you can reduce your risks.

When evaluating how well risk-reduction actions work, check to make sure you can compare the numbers. For example, if you are asked to choose between A: a 1% reduction of a 1 in 100 lifetime risk and B: a 1% reduction of a 1 in 10,000 lifetime risk, then consider rewriting these as:

A: Going from 1,000 to 990 in 100,000 (a reduction of 10 out of 100,000)
B: Going from 10 to 9.9 in 100,000 (a reduction of 0.1 out of 100,000)

Which of the following actions would you view as better (all else being equal)?
1. Reducing the same risk from 2 in 10,000 to 1 in 10,000 or from 15 in 100,000 to 10 in 100,000?
2. Doing something that increases annual risk by 1 in 1,000 or lifetime risk by 1 in 1,000?
3. Reducing an absolute risk of 1 in 100 by a factor of 2 or an absolute risk of 1 in 10,000 by a factor of 100?

Exercise 7: Checking Ranges and Confidence

Researchers generally report their findings as expected values within a range. The breadth of the range (the precision) shows their confidence about the results. A narrow range indicates that the researchers are very confident in their results, while a wide range indicates little confidence. If the range is excessively wide, then the information may be accurate but not very helpful. Alternatively, if the range is excessively narrow, the information may not be very accurate. In particular, people are known to be overly precise (or overconfident) when asked for information. For example, when asked to answer questions for which they do not know the answer, most people will offer a single number instead of a range. This leads them to be exactly wrong, while offering a range might allow them to be approximately right.

Sources can report single numbers in ways that are very misleading. Typically reporters pull numbers out of a range and they do not inform you about the researcher's confidence in the result. When faced with a single number, you need to understand whether the number reflects the worst case, the best case, or something in the middle. For example, scientists might project based on previous years that between 40,000 and 50,000 Americans will die this year in motor vehicle accidents with a best guess of 45,000. If one report based on the lowest number says "Deaths from vehicles expected to exceed 40,000" and another report based on the highest number says "Up to 50,000 motor vehicle deaths possible" then the information from the two reports could appear to differ by 10,000 lives and conflict when in fact they simply span the range of scientific uncertainty.

The most important test of the quality of information is whether it represents the truth. Does the source usually provide valid information? You can test the accuracy of your local weather information by comparing the actual measured temperatures and precipitation to predictions. Or, make your own predictions about some future events and see how well you do at predicting the outcomes. When you evaluate sources, think about the accuracy of their earlier predictions.

Finally, note that information about only the range tells you nothing about how likely the numbers within the range are to occur. For example, note the big difference between hearing that any temperature between -40 and 200 ^{O}F is equally likely to occur and hearing that the forecaster is 99.99% certain that tomorrow's high temperature will be between 70 and 80 ^{O}F and 0.01% certain that the temperature will lie outside that range. You should seek information about the chances of any particular number occurring.

Do you tend to give overconfident answers to questions when you're uncertain? The following questions can help you assess your tendency to provide overconfident estimtates. For each question, give your best estimate, and your 80% confidence interval. Thus, for the lower bound, estimate the number for which you judge only a 10% chance exists that the true value is lower, and for the upper bound, estimate the number for which you judge only a 10% chance exists that the true value is higher. You should guess without looking up the answers elsewhere.

1. In the United States in 2002, what percentage of households owned their own home?
Best estimate _____ Lower bound _____ Upper bound _____

2. In the United States in 1999, out of every 100 live births how many babies weighed less than 1,500 grams?
Best estimate _____ Lower bound _____ Upper bound _____

3. In the United States in 1999, what was life expectancy at birth (in years) for females?
Best estimate _____ Lower bound _____ Upper bound _____

4. What percentage of the United States population had Internet access in 2001?
Best estimate _____ Lower bound _____ Upper bound _____

5. In 1999 in the United States, what was the ratio of the number of cancer deaths to the number of heart disease deaths?
Best estimate _____ Lower bound _____ Upper bound _____

6. What was the median annual household income in the United States in 2001?
Best estimate _____ Lower bound _____ Upper bound _____

7. In 2000 in the United States, what percentage of black males aged 18-24 were smokers?
Best estimate _____ Lower bound _____ Upper bound _____

8. How many tons of coal did the United States burn in 2002 to generate electricity?
Best estimate _____ Lower bound _____ Upper bound _____

9. In 1998 in the United States, what percent of people were covered by health insurance for the entire year?
Best estimate _____ Lower bound _____ Upper bound _____

10. How many people died from motor vehicle accidents in the United States in 2000?
Best estimate _____ Lower bound _____ Upper bound _____

Once you record your answers, go to the AORM web site to go on to the next step (www.aorm.com).

Exercise 8: Adding Context

Consider the role of numbers in the amount of risk and in the distinction between a remedy and a toxin:
1. What happens if you take two aspirin for a headache? What if you take 20 aspirin?
2. What happens if you have one drink? What if you have five drinks?
3. Is someone who spends one hour driving a day less likely to be in a motor vehicle accident than someone who drives nine hours a day?

For each of the following actions that might reduce your risk of dying in a motor vehicle accident, think about your choices and how collective actions impact you:
1. Wearing a safety belt
2. Not speeding
3. Driving defensively
4. Choosing a bigger car
5. Not talking on your cell phone while driving
6. Avoiding alcohol prior to driving
(For example, for number 1, manufacturers put the safety belts in the vehicle. State laws require you to wear a belt - except for people over 18 in New Hampshire where you can "Live free or die" - and penalties come from not obeying the law.)

How would you compare actions with two different types of outcomes?
Which is better:
1. Preventing 1 death from brain cancer or 10 deaths from pancreatic cancer?
2. Preventing 10 deaths from cancer or 10 deaths from heart disease?
3. Preventing 10 cases of severe asthma or 10 cases of severe arthritis?
4. Preventing 10 cases of measles or 100 cases of chicken pox?

Would you choose to make the following trade-offs?
1. Install a $20 smoke detector in your house to warn you in the case of fire
2. Install a $1,000 device to instantly notify someone to send help when you are in danger
3. Leave home 5 minutes earlier to avoid driving to work recklessly
4. Spend 3 hours a week exercising to increase your life expectancy by 1 year
5. Spend $1 every day to buy a lottery ticket, each with a 1 in 10,000,000 chance of winning 1 million dollars? (If you spend $1,000 each year buying lottery tickets your chances of winning are only 1,000 in 10,000,000 or 1 in 10,000. Note that you'd have to spend 10 million dollars to expect to win 1 million dollars given these odds).

Debunked and Uncertain Quotes

While searching for the origins of a number of the quotes, I debunked a couple of my favorite quotes as not verifiable and unlikely to be from the person to whom they are frequently attributed. These include:

"Not everything that counts can be counted, and not everything that can be counted counts." Attributed to Albert Einstein in the Oct. 1977 *Reader's Digest*, but not able to be verified by Alice Calaprice in *The Expanded Quotable Einstein*.

"A lie gets halfway around the world before the truth has a chance to get its pants on." Attributed to Sir Winston Churchill, but probably not said by him.

"I find that the harder I work, the more luck I seem to have." Attributed to Thomas Jefferson, but probably not said by him.

The following list provides some great quotes whose origins I could not confirm by looking in reputable sources, so use them AT YOUR OWN RISK and EXPRESS UNCERTAINTY ABOUT THEIR ORIGIN! The list includes the names to which the quotes are frequently attributed. I will post any information that I receive about the origins of these on the Age of Risk Management web site (www.aorm.com), so if you can resolve the uncertainty and provide the original citation for any of these then quotes please let me know.

"In theory, there is no difference between theory and practice. But, in practice, there is." Attributed to Jan L.A. van de Snepscheut

"Don't be afraid to take a big step if one is indicated; you can't cross a chasm in two small jumps." Attributed to David Lloyd George

"Once I make up my mind, I'm full of indecision." Attributed to Oscar Levant

"Deliver me from the man who never makes a mistake, and also from the man who makes the same mistake twice." Attributed to Dr. William Mayo

"One of the advantages of being disorderly is that one is constantly making exciting discoveries." Attributed to Alan Alexander Milne

"Death has this consolation: it frees us from the thoughts of death." Attributed to Jules Renard

"Most people would sooner die than think; in fact, they do so." Attributed to Bertrand Russell

"When you do the common things in life in an uncommon way, you will command the attention of the world." Attributed to George Washington Carver

"The only man with anything to say is the man of science, and he can't say it." Attributed to James M. Barrie

"A conclusion is the place where you got tired of thinking." Attributed to Martin A. Fischer

"Today's science is tomorrow's technology." Attributed to Edward Teller

"The trouble with our times is that the future is not what it used to be." Attributed to Paul Valéry

"Home was quite a place when people stayed home." Attributed to E.B. White

"Deep-seated preferences cannot be argued about: you cannot argue a man into liking a glass of beer." Attributed to Oliver Wendell Holmes

"I don't know much about medicine, but I do know what I like." Attributed to S. Perelman

"I'd rather attempt something great and fail than attempt nothing and succeed." Attributed to Robert H. Schuller

"The average man does not know what to do with this life, yet wants another one which will last forever." Attributed to Anatole France

"Remember that the conquest of glory exceeds the glory of conquest." Attributed to Leonardo DaVinci

"A people that values its privileges above its principles soon loses both." Attributed to Dwight D. Eisenhower

"University politics are vicious precisely because the stakes are so small." Attributed to Henry Kissinger

"I am dying with the help of too many physicians." Attributed to Alexander, the Great

"Attention to health is life's greatest hindrance." Attributed to Plato

"Happiness is good health and a bad memory." Attributed to Ingrid Bergman

"If everything seems under control, you're just not going fast enough." Attributed to Mario Andretti

"The man of science does not discover in order to know; he wants to know in order to discover." Attributed to A.N. Whitehead

About the Author

At the time of publication, Dr. Kimberly M. Thompson served as Associate Professor of Risk Analysis and Decision Science at the Harvard School of Public Health, where she created and directed the Kids Risk Project. She wrote *Overkill: How Our Nation's Abuse of Antibiotics and Other Germ Killers Is Hurting Your Health and What You Can Do About It* with Debra Bruce (Rodale, 2002) and over 50 academic publications covering a wide range of topics from air bags and chemicals to vaccines and video games.

Dr. Thompson created the Age of Risk Management web site (www.AORM.com) to provide links to all of her work. A popular speaker, recognized as a Society for Risk Analysis/Sigma Xi Distinguished Lecturer in 2003, she has appeared on numerous national and international television shows and radio programs. Dr. Thompson's research focuses on children's risks and on using the tools of risk analysis and decision science to empower kids, parents, policy makers, and others to improve their lives. Dr. Thompson earned her Doctor of Science degree from the Harvard School of Public Health and her Bachelor and Master of Science Degrees from the Massachusetts Institute of Technology. At the time of publication, she and her husband were raising their two children and navigating the Age of Risk Management in Newton, MA.

Praise for *Risk in Perspective*:

"This book will be invaluable for anyone who teaches risk analysis, risk assessment, risk management, or risk communication. All courses can use humor, and this book provides humor with strong teaching messages."
John F. Ahearne, PhD, Sigma Xi and Past President of the Society for Risk Analysis

"It's a risky business for an author to attempt a humorous book about risks. It's riskier still to be successful. For the readers of this book, however, there are no risks at all, only the substantial benefits of real laughter - in other words, a highly favorable benefit/risk ratio."
Dennis M. Bier, MD, Director, USDA/ARS Children's Nutrition Research Center, Baylor College of Medicine

"Science has long illustrated the risks inherent in every day living - from driving to taking a shower to even watching the television. In fact, there are more than 3,000 studies analyzing the risks of violent media entertainment and its overall negative impact on our public health. All of this comes down to one critical point: what we feed the mind and soul is even more important than what we feed the body. At last someone understands and has articulated this!"
U.S. Senator Sam Brownback (R-Kansas)

"They're all here: History's greatest philosophers and scientists join today's cartoonists to handle your risk management problems. Laugh and learn with *Risk in Perspective: Insight and Humor in the Age of Risk Management*. You'll laugh, be provoked, humbled, find rapport, think about a cartoon's message, reread a helpful quote, and find it absolutely impossible to put this book down."
Bill Deane, News Editor, CBS News

"Humor is a wonderful catalyst for learning. Kim Thompson's new book has pulled together a virtual menagerie of cartoons that will allow scientists, students, and the public to confront risk management issues with smiles, poignancy, and growing understanding."
Sharon Dunwoody, PhD, Evjue-Bascom Professor of Journalism, University of Wisconsin

"Be warned that there is some risk in reading this book. You'll enjoy the material so much you'll likely experience a growing feeling of guilt. After all, risk is a serious subject, and shouldn't provide so much fun. Imagine, quotes from Twain, Einstein, and Jefferson - and hundreds of cartoons. You can't beat that!"
Sidney Harris, Cartoon Artist, ScienceCartoonsPlus.com

"An insightful, enlightening, educational and entertaining approach to contemporary risk taking behaviors."
Carden Johnston, MD, FAACP, President, American Academy of Pediatrics

"A creative and humorous approach to the ways we respond to risk."
U.S. Senator Joe Lieberman (D-Connecticut)

"Imagine this: A whole book of cartoons about health, organized by risk factors. Who would have ever expected that? Read this book, laugh and learn."
**George Lundberg, MD, Editor, MedGenMed and
Special Healthcare Advisor to the Chairman and CEO of WebMD**

"For anyone interested in risk and decision making this collection of superbly selected cartoons and verbal nuggets is shear delight. I can hardly wait until I can spice up my presentations with a sprinkling of some of these insightful and humorous gems."
Howard Raiffa, Professor Emeritus, Harvard Business School

"As today's consumers wade through the overwhelming amount of health information, this unique book will empower them, motivate them to ask good questions, and leave them smiling along the way. Professor Thompson's book would be enlightening for everyone, and it is destined to become a must-read for all involved in generating, providing, and consuming health information."
Sylvia Rowe, President and CEO, International Food Information Council

"Kim Thompson has captured, along with the cartoonists, the essence of how medical care is delivered and the choices we, as lay consumers, are required to make. Their perspective lends a necessary degree of levity to a very serious subject. Hadassah's *Healthy Women, Healthy Lives* seminars present the issues that are expressed as well in this wonderful new book."
June Walker, President, Hadassah, Women's Zionist Organization of America, Inc.

"Dr. Kimberly M. Thompson's book *Risk in Perspective: Insight and Humor in the Age of Risk Management* invites you to chuckle your way to understanding scientific risk assessment. Dr. Thompson, with her priceless collection of cartoons, quotations and Proverbs surrounded by simple, clear text, will make you both laugh and learn. Even more important, this book will equip you with a new sophistication and skepticism about how to judge the 'health risk de jour' regularly reported on the nightly news."
Elizabeth M . Whelan, ScD, MPH, President, American Council on Science and Health

"Empowering: important messages - enhanced by timeless quotes from famous people - and supported with humorous (and eye-opening) cartoons by nationally recognized artists."
J. Thomas Zender, President, Unity